Contending for the Truth

A Biblical Look at Thirteen Contentious Doctrines

L. J. Anderson

Lamad Press

Copyright © 2025 by L. J. Anderson (originally published as *Parables and Teachings: Understanding God's Truth* by Logan Anderson)

www.ljandersonbooks.com

Published by Lamad Press, PO Box 50785, Billings MT, 59105, www.lamadpress.com

ISBN 978-1-963291-05-6 (hardback), 978-1-963291-04-9 (paperback), and 978-1-963291-03-2 (eBook)

All rights reserved.

No portion of this book may be reproduced in any form without written permission from the publisher or author, except as permitted by US copyright law.

Unless otherwise noted, Scripture quotations are from the ESV® Bible (The Holy Bible, English Standard Version®), © 2001 by Crossway, a publishing ministry of Good News Publishers. Used by permission. All rights reserved.

Book cover by Jenn Anderson

Illustrations by L. J. Anderson

First edition 2025

Contents

Introduction	1
1. Why God?	6
2. The Moral Argument	14
3. Truth	30
4. The Inerrancy of Scripture	43
5. Gnosticism: A Biblical and Historical Response	58
6. Biblical Forgiveness	72
7. Biblical Church Discipline	85
8. Is Christianity a Religion or a Relationship?	98
9. Religious Freedom	108
10. Scientific Naturalism v Creationism	121
11. Young Earth v Old Earth Creationism	133
12. Sons of God	150
13. The Doctrine of Election	166
A Brief Call to Action	184
Also by L. J. Anderson	185
Bibliography	186

INTRODUCTION

While this book is written with a more mature believer in mind, it is my hope that new believers, and even those who are just looking into Christianity, can find value in it. Regardless of what category you fit into, I would like to give you some insight into this book.

This book is primarily for those who have been Christians for a while, have grown in their faith, and desire to continue to grow in their faith. I do not go over many of the basics of the faith as the book assumes the reader already knows these things. Instead, it deals with specific problems or common beliefs/sayings in Christianity that may or may not actually be biblical. Thus, it is designed to be more of a refinement of one's faith rather than a starting point. That said, if you have questions regarding any of these topics or want to know more about the basics of the faith that are not addressed, please feel free to contact me at ljandersonbooks@outlook.com. I welcome questions and will do my best to respond quickly and helpfully to anyone who reaches out.

Entire books have been written about each of the subjects I discuss, so this is not an exhaustive account by any means. My hope is that you will be inspired to study more about these subjects. In addition to engaging with other theologians and demonstrating my own research, I've provided citations throughout this book to give you an idea of some other sources you can look at on these topics. Not all sources I engage with are ones that

I *endorse* as good theology and even if I *do* endorse a specific book that does not mean I believe that it is free from errors. Likewise, while I firmly believe that the contents of this book are the truth, I don't want you to take my word for it. Read what I have written, ask God to help you see and understand the truth, and go to his Word to confirm what you have read. Never take anyone other than God at their word. Everyone, except God, makes mistakes, and sometimes people mislead others on purpose. Thus, it is imperative to do your own research to make sure what you have read agrees with God.

Also, if you are interested, I have my personal testimony on my blog at ljandersonbooks.com. If you would like to read my deepest, darkest secrets, then that is where you should go. You will get snippets of my testimony in some of these chapters, but the whole thing is on my website. While I am saddened that I made the choices that I have made, I am no longer who I once was. I hope you will see that if and when you read my story. God makes all things new!

Additionally, I want to make it clear what my process tends to be when I research a topic. If the topic is focused on Scripture, I begin with Scripture, unlike many scholars/theologians. A typical view of how to write a Christian or biblical research paper can be found in *Surviving and Thriving in Seminary: An Academic and Spiritual Handbook* by H.

Daniel Zacharias and Benjamin K. Forrest.[1] My method is different. Once something piques my interest as I read or think about Scripture, theology, or some other discipline, I compile massive amounts of verses and passages related, or even obliquely related, to the topic. Then I spend significant time trying to understand what is being said about that topic in individual verses and throughout Scripture. This is generally when I begin writing down what Scripture seems to be saying. At this point, I often intentionally avoid reading other people's work, to preclude outside influences. After I have written the chapter/book, or at least have it sketched out, *then* I begin the process of engaging fellow theologians. Has what I gleaned from Scripture been taught before? What, if any, arguments are given against it? I ask these and similar questions to confirm what I have concluded, give me reasons to rethink my conclusions, or address areas that I neglected or failed to convey well. Interestingly, this process has *always* resulted in conclusions that others have already made. Sometimes these conclusions have not been common or, as is the case with my chapter on forgiveness, seem to have not been mainstream for a really long time. Anyone who dives into what Scripture teaches on forgiveness will recognize that the commonly taught method of forgiveness in contemporary Christian circles is wrong.

---

1. H. Daniel Zacharias and Benjamin K. Forrest, *Surviving and Thriving in Seminary: An Academic and Spiritual Handbook* (Bellingham, WA: Lexham Press, 2017), 147-150. I did a review on this book and this concept was one of the things I critiqued. The example they use is "Jesus' teaching on divorce" which should have the *primary* focus on God's Word since that is the topic. What did *Jesus* say about divorce? Yet, on step four, they only write, "Read articles on divorce in Bible dictionaries. Make notes and identify key Bible passages" (pg. 148). The emphasis should be on Scripture rather than scholars' points of view. The book review can be found on my website at https://ljandersonbooks.com/2024/08/16/surviving-and-thriving-in-seminary-an-academic-and-spiritual-handbook-h-daniel-zacharias-and-benjamin-k-forrest-bellingham-wa-lexham-press-2017-book-review-by-l-j-anderson/.

There *are* those who teach true biblical forgiveness, but they just aren't mainstream.

Finally, I want to give a warning. Much of my writing is considered doctrine. Many Christians have a low view of doctrine, considering it divisive. However, *doctrine* is merely *teaching*. Thus, this book is built on biblical *teachings*. Doctrine *can* be negatively divisive, but it can also be positively divisive. We are to "rightly handle the word of truth" (2 Timothy 2:15) and this involves correcting those who *do not* rightly handle the Word of truth.[2] Without doctrine, this is impossible since doctrine is simply teaching what the Bible teaches. That said, one of the biggest challenges with doctrine outside of getting it right, is applying it to our lives. In the majority of the chapters in this book, I end with some possible takeaways from what I am teaching. However, it is up to you to apply what you learn in this book, other books, and Scripture itself to your own life. Studying God's Word and reading theology books is a worthy pursuit, but it is of no value if we do not *learn* from them and then *change* our lives to better align with Christ. James 1:22–25 says,

> Be doers of the word, and not hearers only, deceiving yourselves. For if anyone is a hearer of the word and not a doer, he is like a man who looks intently at his natural face in a mirror. For he looks at himself and goes away and at once forgets what he was like. But the one who looks into the perfect law, the law of liberty, and perseveres, being no hearer

---

2. This correction should be done with love. Additionally, it should be done gently if at all possible. Sometimes though, Scripture demonstrates that harsh consequences need to be applied. See chapter 7 for more information on this.

who forgets but a doer who acts, he will be blessed in his doing.

I pray God will use this book to grow your faith!

A Note About the Second Edition

In 2019, I first published this book under the title *Parables and Teachings: Understanding God's Truth*. After publishing that first edition, I realized the title didn't accurately reflect the content, since it contained few parables, and the chapter lengths were inconsistent. I either needed to rewrite the book to make it better align with the title or change the title to something closer and fill it out to be more consistent. Ultimately, I decided to do the latter, changing out a bunch of the chapters so that it was a more cohesive book while also filling out the chapters that were too short. The result is almost an entirely different book. It is twice as long, has only half of the original chapters, and is more academic than the first edition. Additionally, it is more cohesive, has a completely different title, has a slightly different focus, and, I believe, is better written. All of that made me question why I would consider this a second edition of *Parables and Teachings* rather than its own thing. I ended up considering it a second edition because of two things. First, the concept behind the book has not changed. It is individual teachings pieced together under one title. Second, many of the chapters are on the same topics but have simply been rewritten and expanded. Thus, a second edition would be the most faithful way for me to publish this book even though it is hardly the same book.

Chapter One

Why God?

I DO NOT INTEND this chapter to be a robust defense of the existence of God. Rather, I seek to briefly hit on many of the different arguments for God's existence. Basically, I want to demonstrate that believing in God is actually quite rational without it taking up the entire book. We can logically deduce that the existence of God is the most reasonable answer to many of life's biggest questions. After giving this brief overview, I will engage with a couple of the arguments more in-depth in chapters two and ten.

Why do Christians believe so strongly that there is a God and that their God is the one true God? That is a great question. Unfortunately, it is one that many Christians can't give a satisfactory answer to. Often the answer you will get is something along the lines of "I just believe that God is real." A lot of contemporary Christians just don't care to look into the details as to *why* they believe what they believe so that they can give satisfactory answers to those who ask. What is interesting is that there are a lot of ways we can go about answering this question. We can look at history and verify the Bible by what nonbiblical accounts say. We can look at the fact that no matter how hard people have tried to destroy Christianity, they are never successful. We can look at creation and see how the design behind it all cannot have come about by chance. And we can look at pure logic. I am going to address most of these briefly. Despite this chapter being more of an overview, I hope you will take the time to do some deep thinking on this and, as Gandalf once said, "Bring forth the questions, Frodo," or something like that.

Philosopher Gregory E. Ganssle writes, "The problem of evil is, perhaps, the most common objection to theistic belief."[1] Essentially, the question is this: How could a loving God allow evil? That question can be answered, and I will answer it, but the first thing that should be asked in response is: If there is no God, what is evil? Without the existence of a being that is beyond humans saying, "This is evil," we wouldn't even have an understanding of evil. In fact, nothing that humans do could be considered evil. If we evolved from nothing and are nothing more than animals, then there is no such thing as evil. While discussing the apologist Fyodor Dostoyevsky's take on the human predicament, renowned contemporary Christian apologist and philosopher William Lane Craig notes, "If the existence of God is denied, then one is landed in complete moral relativism, so that no act, regardless how dreadful or heinous, can be condemned by the atheist."[2] Survival of the fittest is natural in the world of animals so why do we say that it is evil when the strong kill or exert their wills on the weak? That is merely a natural reaction, right? The strong survive and the weak perish. Why do we, as humans, care about the weak? Why do we care about those who go hungry, those who are raped, or those who are murdered? Why do we care about justice being served for these crimes? Evil cannot

---

1. Paul Copan and Paul K. Moser, eds., *The Rationality of Theism* (New York: Routledge, 2003), 259.

2. William Lane Craig, *Reasonable Faith: Christian Truth and Apologetics* (Wheaton, IL: Crossway, 2008), 69.

exist without a higher authority (God) declaring something to be wrong. Evil is simply anything counter to God's design.[3]

Now back to the original question: How could a loving God allow evil? Stuart Goetz states, "The argument from or problem of evil concludes that the existence of evil is, in one way or another, incompatible with the existence of an omnipotent, omnibenevolent, and omniscient being (God)."[4] Despite how commonly it's asked, this question has always struck me as odd. I believe that most people who ask it don't think through the consequences of what a "loving" God who *doesn't* allow evil would look like. He would simply be a puppet master. Humans would have no free will to do anything, good or bad. This is precisely the reason the tree of the knowledge of good and evil was in the Garden of Eden, so that we had the *choice* to obey or disobey God. It gave mankind the ability to choose good or evil. Humans have shown that we always choose to disobey on some level or another. Thus, we are the cause of much of the evil in the world. To be sure, we aren't the only ones causing evil things to happen. Satan and his demons are doing all they can to prevent people from turning to God and being forces for good. Also, bad things happen because we live in a fallen creation. When Adam and Eve chose to sin against God, God said, "Cursed is the ground because of you" in Genesis 3:17. Therefore, creation is fallen and accounts for some of the bad things that happen. At no point, does God desire for us to obey him unwillingly. To force humans

---

3. This is a major portion of the moral argument which will be addressed in greater detail in the next chapter. Additionally, for further reading, consider David Baggett and Jerry L. Walls' *The Moral Argument* and/or C. S. Lewis's *Mere Christianity*.

4. William Lane Craig and J. P. Moreland, eds, *The Blackwell Companion to Natural Theology* (Malden, MA: Blackwell Publishing, 2012), 449.

to do good is about as *unloving* as it gets. Thus, a *loving* God *must* allow evil, at least for a time. One day, when Jesus returns, evil and suffering will be no more (Revelation 21:4). Until then, God allows evil its place.

This brings us to humans specifically. Many people will argue that humans are basically good. That is, quite simply, an outrageous statement. Humans are the ones that have perpetrated all the mass murders, genocides, rapes, thefts, and all other types of evil acts done throughout the history of mankind. We are selfish, liars, adulterers, idolaters, greedy, and drunkards. Of course, there are many examples of humans doing amazing things for the good of others. We are wired to desire justice and want to live good lives. This is part of what it means to be created in God's image. We demonstrate that we have the law of God written on our hearts. Despite this overall desire to live well, we constantly miss the mark. Believe it or not, we *also* desire to do exactly as we want. We desire to be our own gods. In some cases, the desire to live morally gets pushed down enough by people that they become willing and active participants in evil.[5] What ends up happening is that we blame our evil desires on other people or things. For example, in recent years, guns have been portrayed as evil and not the people using them. Yet a gun is a neutral tool. There is nothing evil about a gun because it is an inanimate object that has no will. It is the *user* who determines what happens with a gun. Beginning with the first humans, Adam and Eve, mankind has played this blame game of pushing responsibility off onto someone or something else. Genesis 3:11–13 says,

---

5. Hitler, serial killers, and Epstein are examples of people who have (or had) given themselves over to sin.

> He [God] said, "Who told you that you were naked? Have you eaten of the tree of which I commanded you not to eat?" The man said, "The woman whom you gave to be with me, she gave me fruit of the tree, and I ate." Then Yahweh God said to the woman, "What is this that you have done?" The woman said, "The serpent deceived me, and I ate."[6]

Notice what happened there? The first two humans to ever walk the earth did evil, and *both* of them blamed it on something or someone else. Adam blamed Eve and, if you read the passage closely enough, he blamed *God*. Eve blamed the serpent. Of course, the serpent *did* deserve some of the blame, which we see in verses 14 and 15. God didn't let the serpent off the hook. That said, Adam and Eve are more to blame since they knew what God's command was, yet they still disobeyed. This blame game is still happening today.

What about life's purpose? Every human desires to live a good and purposeful life. Unfortunately, without God, there is no purpose to life. We live, we pay taxes, and then we die. That's it. As Ben Franklin said, "In

---

6. All Old Testament references to the divine name are written as "Yahweh." The verses quoted in this book are from the ESV, but I am unwilling to obscure God's name to appease a tradition of men—even a tradition that began with good intentions. The most used word in the entire Bible, if one discounts pronouns and similar words, is "Yahweh." In fact, it is used nearly 7,000 times which indicates its importance. We would do well to remember to give God's name its proper weight. To not do so, is to take the name of Yahweh in vain (Exodus 20:7). This verse essentially means that we are not to make the name of Yahweh worthless. In an attempt to avoid the judgment of the third of the ten commandments, the Jews refused to speak the name of Yahweh. By doing so they made his name *worthless* because they forgot what it was. I will not make the same mistake. This is a personal conviction that I believe has significant merit. God gives great weight to his name, and I cannot go against him by lessening it.

this world, nothing can be said to be certain, except death and taxes."[7] A universe that came about by chance cannot give us a greater purpose. If we evolved out of nothing, then there is no purpose and no meaning in life. Survival is the only thing that matters, and even that is questionable as to whether it truly matters under evolution.

What about how life started? Or even earlier than that, what about how the universe came to be? How can the universe come from nothing? Or if it didn't come from nothing, how could the "stuff" in the universe come to be? Even most secular scientists have to agree that the universe had a definite start. Their timeline might be completely different from a creationist's timeline, but they agree that the universe isn't eternal, for nothing natural can be eternal. All natural things have a beginning and an end. Thus, for something to have come from nothing, we would need something more than just "natural" causes. We would need a supernatural being who is outside of time. Interestingly, God *is* a supernatural being who is outside of time. There was no time until God created it. I will admit that this idea is beyond our comprehension because a finite mind cannot truly understand something that has no beginning and no end. Yet, the existence of an eternal supernatural being is the only thing that makes logical sense for how the universe came into being. Every other option always runs into the question: And where did *that* come from? The typical claim is that the universe was a very dense ball of gas and dust prior to the Big Bang, but where did the gas and dust come from? Any answer to that question apart from "God" leads again to the same question. At

---

7. Alexander Engel, "'In This World Nothing Can Be Said to Be Certain, except Death and Taxes' Benjamin Franklin, 1789," *Colorectal Disease*, April 1, 2012. https://doi.org/10.1111/j.1463-1318.2012.03001.x.

some point, this line of reasoning leads inevitably to claim that everything came from nothing which, as already noted, is impossible. On the flip side, atheists often use this line of questioning against God despite him being the only being/thing that can legitimately claim to have no beginning.[8]

Along the same lines, there is simply too much complexity and too much order in the universe for it to have come about by chance. Contemporary Christian philosopher Del Ratzsch writes, "Activities of human agents typically leave visible traces on the world—traces we are generally able to recognize as resulting from human activity."[9] As we would typically recognize the work of fellow humans even if the humans themselves have moved on, so too we can recognize a designer of the universe even if we cannot physically see the designer himself. Despite all of our technology, we can't make even the most basic cell, and yet many believe that the same cell could form by chance when there was no life present. There has been research done into synthesizing cells, but no cell has been made from scratch. Nor will it ever happen. Replacing DNA in already-made cells is the closest we will ever get. The way that secular science gets around the problem of complexity is by throwing millions, if not billions, of years at it. The theory is that life, and then complex life, must happen *eventually* given enough time. Yet the odds of life happening in the first place are astronomical. So many things have to come together *perfectly* in order to have a functional universe, much less a functioning universe with *life*. This is called "cosmic fine-tuning." William Lane Craig, writes, "By 'fine-tuning' one means that small deviations from the actual values of the constants

---

8. A discussion on the origins of the universe is dealt with in greater detail in chapter 10.

9. Khaldoun A. Sweis and Chad V. Meister, *Christian Apologetics: An Anthology of Primary Sources* (Grand Rapids, MI: Zondervan, 2012), 472.

and quantities in question would render the universe life-prohibiting or, alternatively, that the range of life-permitting values is exquisitely narrow in comparison with the range of assumable values."[10] There are many cases of fine-tuning. For example, if the force of the gravitational constant was only slightly stronger or slightly weaker, the universe wouldn't function in a way that is conducive to life. If it were slightly stronger, the stars would burn at a much quicker rate and would be much smaller. If it were slightly weaker, the stars and planets couldn't form in the first place.

Additionally, the theory of evolution espouses that order came from disorder. This belief is in direct conflict with the prevailing science. What we actually see in science is that the world and the universe don't go from disorder to order, rather it does the exact opposite. The second law of thermodynamics says that entropy increases with time in a closed system. Entropy is a decline into disorder. This means that we can't expect an unordered system to morph into an ordered system without some sort of outside influence. Again, we will dig into this idea quite a bit more in chapter 10.

All of this goes to show that there *must* be a God who created everything. It takes more faith to say everything in the universe happened by chance than it does to believe that there is a God. As much as I don't like using that argument because it has a misunderstanding of what "faith" is and it is rather cliché at this point, it rings true. All of this is without taking into account personal experience with God at the individual level. God is simply the most logical answer to most, if not all, of the questions regarding life and origins in this universe.

---

10. Craig, *Reasonable Faith*, 158.

Chapter Two

The Moral Argument

In many ways, early Christianity, including Scripture itself, was focused on demonstrating that the God of the Bible is the one true God. This is because most of human history has been characterized by theism. It was exceedingly rare for someone in ancient times to have been an atheist. However, in the last few hundred years this has shifted. Atheism and agnosticism are now more prevalent than ever; thus the argumentation has needed to shift from proving that the God of the Bible is the one true God to proving that God exists to begin with. Many methods and arguments have been produced to attempt to prove this with one such attempt being called the moral argument.

The moral argument for God's existence tends to be more popular among non-scholarly Christians than those who are professional scholars/theologians. On the moral argument, theologian John Feinberg states, "This kind of argument isn't as popular among philosophers (even Christian ones) as the others, but it is very appealing to ordinary people. There is a certain commonsense plausibility to it, as one can attest from C. S. Lewis's version in *Mere Christianity*."[1] Feinberg goes on to say that, of all the rational arguments for God, the moral argument is "least likely"

---

1. John S. Feinberg, *No One Like Him: The Doctrine of God* (Wheaton, IL: Crossway, 2005), 199.

to be rationally compelling.[2] Does this mean that the moral argument is not worth pursuing when trying to convince nonbelievers about the existence of God? Is this even a fair representation of the moral argument? Interestingly, many contemporary theologians, who would now dispute Feinberg on this, view this lack of emphasis on the moral argument as a travesty. That said, it remains a rather unreputable argument for God's existence among academics. Despite its mediocre reputation in academic circles, this chapter will demonstrate that the moral argument is one of the most powerful tools for proving the reasonableness of God's existence, especially when paired with other arguments.

History of the Moral Argument

Before engaging with the moral argument itself, it is necessary to look at a brief history of it. This history can fairly effectively be split into two categories, pre-Kant and post-Kant. This is because many would argue that the eighteenth-century German philosopher Immanuel Kant invented, or at least initially systematized, the moral argument for the existence of God.

History Pre-Kant

Immanuel Kant may be the first person to deal with the moral argument systematically enough to be considered its originator. However, there were flavors of this argument as far back as Socrates, Plato, and Aristotle. Philosophy professors and authors David Baggett and Jerry Walls write, "We find in Plato the notion that things have goodness insofar as they stand in some relation to the Good. The Good, Plato believed, subsists

---

2. Ibid., 202. Feinberg argues here that the main value of the moral argument is bolstering a Christian's faith rather than being a convincing argument for taking an atheist from unbelief to belief in God.

in itself."³ This is essentially the view of Christianity only in Christianity the "Good" is the "good God, Yahweh." This idea can be found moving through significant historical Christian figures such as Augustine and Thomas Aquinas.⁴ Other more modern philosophers took up various attempts at a moral argument which finally culminated in Immanuel Kant engaging with it in a major way.

Development Post-Kant

Since Kant first engaged heavily with the moral argument, there has been a back-and-forth between upholding the moral argument as worthwhile and thus developing it (as can be seen in C. S. Lewis's *Mere Christianity*) and holding the argument in such contempt that it was entirely ignored in many apologetics books (such as Alvin Plantinga's *God and Other Minds: A Study of the Rational Justification of Belief in God*). *Mere Christianity* is arguably the most famous attempt at a moral argument. However, it has also been met with criticism that is, in many ways, unfair.⁵ William Lane Craig views the moral argument as the most effective argument for reaching his audiences at college and university campuses based on the response to it.⁶ Non-scholarly Christians have fairly consistently

---

3. David Baggett and Jerry L. Walls, *The Moral Argument: A History* (New York: Oxford University Press, 2019), 9.

4. Ibid., 11.

5. Christopher A. Shrock, "Mere Christianity and the Moral Argument for the Existence of God," *Sehnsucht: The C. S. Lewis Journal* 11, no. 1 (2023): 99-103. https://web.p.ebscohost.com/ehost/pdfviewer/pdfviewer?vid=3&sid=9fffc152-0aac-427a-9b3a-e71bbc550d02%40redis.

6. Baggett and Walls, *The Moral Argument*, 2.

accepted it as worthwhile, and there seems to be a resurgence of it among Christian scholars.

Objections to the Moral Argument

There are three main objections to the moral argument, and they, generally, come from non-Christians. However, there are Christian philosophers who agree that these objections are valid, or at least provide enough reason not to pursue the moral argument as a good argument for the existence of God.

There Are No Universal Objective Morals

In contemporary times, this is likely the most common reasoning against the moral argument. Moral relativism—the view that each culture develops its own morals—holds sway in most Western countries. The fact that many morals seem to be shared by many different cultures is simply the result of human reason recognizing that certain things such as murder are not beneficial for society. There is no overarching power in the universe and one's truth is one's truth even if it runs counter to another person's truth. That said, there are different types of moral relativism. What is described above is a more traditional type similar to what you are likely to run into on the street. Some moral relativists, though, espouse the possibility that universal morals have come about through the process of natural selection as laid out in evolutionary theory.

Objective Morals Can Be Explained Naturalistically

The moral argument states that the only valid explanation for objective morals is some higher power that institutes a law that is above every other law. This can be a non-divine power in that a sufficiently advanced alien race could technically do this if they managed to unlock the ability to create life and instill it with these objective truths. Contrarily, since the nineteenth century, the common view of pretty much anything related to science and humanity comes from an evolutionary angle.[7] Everything has come about by natural, selective processes. The counterargument is that objective morals can come about via naturalistic methods. For example, anthropologists Oliver Curry, Daniel Mullins, and Harvey Whitehouse work toward proving a theory that suggests morals come about from the need to work together for mutual survival. They effectively demonstrated that sixty diverse communities across the world all hold seven moral beliefs universally.[8] This is interesting in that it is a relativistic theory that recognizes the problems with traditional moral relativism. As opposed to traditional moral relativism, this theory holds that there *are* universal morals and has demonstrated this quite effectively.

Begging the Question (On Both Sides)

Both sides of the debate regarding whether there are indeed universal, objective morals accuse the other of begging the question. Begging the question is a logical fallacy wherein someone argues for a specific conclusion based on a preconceived belief in the truth of the said conclusion. For example, I could say "Pineapple doesn't belong on pizza because pizza doesn't have pineapples." This is an extremely simplified example, but

---

7. Dale Eugene Kratt, "The Secular Moral Project and the Moral Argument for God: A Brief Synopsis History," *Religions* 14, no. 8 (2023): 985. https://www.mdpi.com/2077-1444/14/8/982#:~:text=This%20article%20provides%20an%20overview%20of%20the%20history,that%20have%20contributed%20to%20the%20secularization%20of%20ethics.

8. Oliver Scott Curry, Daniel Austin Mullins, and Harvey Whitehouse, "Is It Good to Cooperate? Testing the Theory of Morality-as-Cooperation in 60 Societies," *Current Anthropology* 60:1 (2019): 54.

it demonstrates the point well enough. I need to provide *evidence* that demonstrates pineapple does not belong on pizza in order to logically make the claim that pineapple does not, indeed, belong on pizza. Similarly, from the secular viewpoint, the argument is that Christians only believe in universal morals because Christians already believe in God who created everything, made humans in his image, and is, himself, moral. Thus, Christians *assume* the existence of these universal morals based on the preconceived notion of the existence of a personal divine being. On the flip side, Christians accuse secularists of assuming that there are no universal morals because of their belief that everything came about by chance and natural processes. This challenge is often brought up as an impassible problem for the moral argument.[9] Contemporary Christian philosopher Dale Eugene Kratt exposes one particularly difficult barrier in the dialog between Christians and secularists: "Many current secular thinkers refuse to engage with the theistic arguments or even acknowledge the history of the moral argument."[10] This is similar to the tendency to simply *ignore* the arguments and evidence from young earth creationists. It is hard to engage in debates with those who beg the question so much that they will not even engage with the opposing side.

Counter Arguments and Strengths of the Moral Argument

The previous section demonstrated some of the major objections raised regarding the moral argument, but are these objections valid? The evidence

---

9. Feinberg, *No One Like Him*, 202.

10. Kratt, "The Secular Moral Project," 983.

suggests that the objections are not enough to reject the moral argument as a means of demonstrating the existence of God. Before hitting individual points, it is important to point out the discrepancy that can be seen in the lives of many who argue against universal, objective morals and instead hold to subjectivism in that they are often "later found promoting some moral cause."[11] Many of the most ardent moral relativists also hold certain moral positions as absolute despite the contradiction with their stated beliefs on moralism. Another point of order before getting into specifics is what exactly is meant by "objective" moral values. William Lane Craig gives a good definition when he writes, "To say that there are objective moral values is to say that something is good or evil independently of whether any human being believes it to be so."[12] This is true; however, it is also important to note that objective moral values tend to be universally held except in very rare cases.

Significant Evidence for Universal Objective Morals

Universal, objective morals are not rare. In some sense, they are so obvious that most people do not even think twice about them. C. S. Lewis argues the case for objective morals by saying,

> But taking the race as a whole [as opposed to finding individual exceptions], they thought that the human idea of decent behavior was obvious to everyone. And I believe they were right. If they were not, then all the things we said about the war were nonsense. What was the sense of saying the enemy were in the wrong unless Right is a real thing which the Nazis

---

11. Craig and Moreland, *The Blackwell Companion*, 394.

12. Craig, *Reasonable Faith*, 258.

at the bottom knew as well as we did and ought to have practiced?[13]

The whole fight against the Nazis was predicated on the knowledge that what they were doing was morally wrong. Interestingly, when Nazi leaders began to be tried for their crimes, their defense lawyers argued for moral relativism (the idea that morality is determined by culture with no universals) and this defense was almost insurmountable in an era where moral relativism was taking a greater hold on the world. Philosophy professor and author J. P. Moreland states, "Individuals following the trial were shocked by how effective the Nazis' defense team was in arguing against the charges. How is that possible? What defense could be given for the indefensible?"[14] Ultimately, their defense was only defeated by appealing to a "law above the law."[15]

Many different areas can be looked at to demonstrate these universally understood moral beliefs. One area is found in a study that attempted to prove the morality-as-cooperation theory. This study found, "In 961 out of 962 observations (99.9%), cooperative behavior had a positive moral

---

13. C. S. Lewis, *Mere Christianity* (New York: HarperOne, 1952), 5.

14. J. P. Moreland, *Love Your God with All Your Mind: The Role of Reason in the Life of the Soul* (Colorado Springs: NavPress, 2012), 188.

15. Ibid.

valence."[16] The study did not test for any other areas of morality; however, the fact remains that certain things are universally held as morally good and things contrary to these are universally immoral.[17]

Murder is another area that demonstrates a rather universal view, morally speaking. Justin Hogan-Doran, a senior counsel of the Australian Bar and an arbitrator in international and domestic arbitrations, states, "Whilst the crime of murder, and its equivalents, is clearly defined and subject to extensive jurisprudence in every jurisdiction, no attempt has been made to give this crime a definition at the international level."[18] The fact that a country makes something illegal does not necessarily mean that it is immoral; however, the fact that *every* jurisdiction understands murder as a problem that *needs* to be illegal suggests that murder is a universal, objective, moral evil. You could ask essentially anyone anywhere in the world whether it is wrong to murder someone and in almost all instances the answer to the question will be an emphatic "yes." Of course, the fact

---

16. Curry, Mullins, and Whitehouse, "Is It Good to Cooperate?" 54. This article found that the seven areas that they specifically tested for (helping family members, helping group members, engaging in reciprocal cooperation, being brave, respecting one's superiors, sharing or dividing a disputed resource, and respecting others' property) were universally held as morally good and that the opposites of these things were universally seen as morally bad.

17. Not testing for other areas is a distinct problem with this article as it concludes that the morality-as-cooperation theory is sound even though there are other examples of universal morals that do not necessarily fit under the theory. Thus, the theory does not adequately deal with the various aspects of morality that need to be addressed when discussing the origins of morality.

18. Justin Hogan-Doran, "Case Analysis: Murder as a Crime Under International Law and the Statute of the International Criminal Tribunal for the Former Yugoslavia: Of Law, Legal Language, and a Comparative Approach to Legal Meaning," *Leiden Journal of International Law* 11 (1998): 165.

that murder happens means that humans are able to find ways of *justifying* the wrong, at least in their own heads. An interesting case study on this is the debate surrounding abortion. It is predicated on what constitutes a *human life*. The argument is never that we should have the right to murder. Instead, it is that the child in the womb is not, in fact, a person. As such, pro-abortion advocates sidestep their knowledge that murder is wrong by depersoning babies in the womb. Statements such as "It's only a clump of cells" are common. This allows a disconnect between murder and killing a fetus. Norman L. Geisler writes, "The pro-abortion position is dependent on the belief that the unborn is not an actual human person."[19] Thus, the debate must necessarily revolve around what constitutes a human being. If it can be proven that babies in the womb are, in fact, human, then it is immediately evident that it is murder and thus wrong. Of course, this runs into the distinct problem of people being unwilling to acknowledge the truth. When everyone can have and does have their own "truth," it is less reasonable to consider other points of view as being potentially valid. This is a direct product of the prevalence of moral relativism in Western society.

Naturalistic Explanations Fail on Numerous Counts

Naturalism cannot provide a good basis for any form of universal, objective morals simply because naturalism is necessarily a process of random chance and is subject to the idea of survival of the fittest. Apologist Paul Copan argues, "It is *theism* that furnishes the metaphysical resources to make sense of the instantiation of moral properties in the form of

---

19. Norman L. Geisler, *Christian Ethics: Contemporary Issues & Options* (Grand Rapids, MI: Baker Academic, 2010), 132.

objective moral values, human dignity, human rights, and obligations."[20] A God who made humans in his own image, including knowing right from wrong, is the more logical approach to this problem. It allows for a solid foundation for objective morals which other nontheistic, or even non-personal theistic, theories cannot provide.[21]

Another problem is that those who hold to naturalism tend to uphold the inherent goodness of humans. This view purports that humans can and will achieve a utopia through the power of reason and scientific advancements. Similar to the previous argument, there is no *basis* for this belief. How are humans inherently good? At best, the natural world could produce humans that are inherently *neutral* moralistically speaking. In the animal kingdom, a king snake eating another snake is not *wrong*, it just *is*. However, the vast majority of humans are actively repulsed by the idea of eating another human. Why? Naturalism cannot sufficiently explain why this would be a problem. Killing and eating another human from a Christian perspective though is morally wrong because people are created in the image of God and thus have inherent value. From a naturalist angle, one could correctly argue that a serial killer who goes about killing "rival" males to take their wives as his own is not doing anything wrong. In fact, the killer would be demonstrating natural selection at its finest.

Dealing with the Begging-the-Question Problem

As mentioned previously, the begging-the-question problem of the moral argument is often seen as impassable. However, this is *exactly* how science is supposed to work. One is to come up with a hypothesis that can

---

20. Copan and Moser, *The Rationality of Theism*, 153.

21. Andrew Ter Ern Loke, "A New Moral Argument for the Existence of God," *International Journal for Philosophy of Religion* 93, no. 1 (February 2023): 26.

then be tested. The challenge is *not* that the initial hypothesis is made based on different factors. The problem lies in the willingness to accept evidence and the different interpretations of the results. The two above sections demonstrate, quite well, that the evidence is for the existence of God and against naturalistic explanations. The naturalistic view of morality should look precisely like what is seen in the animal kingdom. The strong rule and the weak perish. Yet, humans are not like this. Humans, as a general rule, *yearn* for justice to be done. People are driven to anger, fury, indignation, and sorrow when the weak and innocent are harmed. This is true in almost every situation. It is, fundamentally, not begging the question to have different hypotheses based on differing beliefs. In the initial discussion of this problem, I gave an example of begging the question in the form of pineapple belonging on pizza. If we were to take that same example and look at it from a different angle, I can *hypothesize* that pineapple does not belong on pizza simply because I do not like it. However, I then need to back that hypothesis up by looking at the evidence of what makes something a *pizza*. I would argue that, though I hate pineapple on pizza, there is no evidence that reasonably precludes pineapple from being on a pizza. My hypothesis, then, should change based on the evidence. This does not typically happen. For example, the morality-as-cooperation theory article discussed above hypothesizes that certain moral traits will be universally seen and that this would prove the viability of the theory. However, the writers fail to do a broad enough search on universal moral attributes. It only takes one universal attribute that is *not* connected to the idea of cooperation to demonstrate that the theory is insufficient. Yet, the authors do not look at other possible moral attributes. Going back to the idea that murder is considered morally wrong universally, we can see that murder does not fit in their seven tested areas.[22] In fact, we can argue that murder being a universal moral belief goes *against* the theory because murdering outsiders is likely to be beneficial in many of the seven areas they tested. If someone is harassing my family members, I should be able to kill the person to help my family members out. However, this is *wrong* and arguably everyone knows it. The writers are so focused on proving the theory that they cannot see the holes in the theory.[23] *That* is the problem, not the fact that we approach the problem with different hypotheses and theories.

Biblical Backing

One of the major strengths of the moral argument is its biblical backing. Often arguments for the existence of God have little to no reference to Scripture as they are philosophical in nature and are often only based on the use of reason. That said, the moral argument is, in many ways, founded on what God himself has said. Of course, this can be seen as a negative thing as so often the argument is assumed to be invalid if Scripture is brought in. However, scriptural support should give Christians confidence to use the argument. Romans 1:18–23 says,

> For the wrath of God is revealed from heaven against all ungodliness and unrighteousness of men, who by their unrighteousness suppress the truth. For what can be known about God is plain to them, because God has shown it to them. For

---

22. To reiterate, these are helping family members, helping group members, engaging in reciprocal cooperation, being brave, respecting one's superiors, sharing or dividing a disputed resource, and respecting others' property.

23. This is why it is helpful to engage with people with different backgrounds and beliefs as it can help us see past the areas that are blocking our vision.

> his invisible attributes, namely, his eternal power and divine nature, have been clearly perceived, ever since the creation of the world, in the things that have been made. So they are without excuse. For although they knew God, they did not honor him as God or give thanks to him, but they became futile in their thinking, and their foolish hearts were darkened. Claiming to be wise, they became fools, and exchanged the glory of the immortal God for images resembling mortal man and birds and animals and creeping things.

This passage directly states that *everyone* knows there is a God; however, some suppress the truth by their unrighteousness. There will always be people who reject the sound understanding that God is the most reasonable explanation for the origin of the universe and life in general, but more specifically, there will always be people who reject that moral absolutes are, in fact, absolute. Scripture tells Christians that everyone knows, deep down, that there is a God. Likewise, everyone knows deep down that there are universal, objective morals. This is also in Scripture. Romans 2:14–15 says,

> For when Gentiles, who do not have the law, by nature do what the law requires, they are a law unto themselves, even though they do not have the law. They show that the work of the law is written on their hearts, while their conscience also bears witness, and their conflicting thoughts accuse or even excuse them.

Gentiles, those who have not received the law, do the law *by nature* because it is *written on their hearts*. Thus, the reason murder is almost universally acknowledged as evil is that God's law, which states that murder is wrong, is written on everyone's heart. This is beneficial for us to know when giving the moral argument. The ones we are talking to *have* God's law written on their hearts. Whether they acknowledge said law is another question; however, we can reasonably expect that they know right from wrong, at least in a basic form. This is often described as the "natural law."

Application

How does the moral argument help Christians live out their lives as Christians? Is it truly valuable for someone to spend their time learning this enough to be able to use it or teach it? Additionally, if one does learn it, should it be used on its own or with other arguments for the existence of God?

The most obvious application of the moral argument is for evangelism. Learning the moral argument is valuable in demonstrating the reasonableness of the existence of God. As with other arguments or methods of evangelism, it is *not* a guaranteed way to evangelize. You and I cannot lay out the moral argument so well that our listeners cannot help but to believe in God. However, it is a valuable way to attempt to reach non-believers for Christ or at least to begin the process of moving some from being an atheist or agnostic to being a theist.

The second area that the moral argument is valuable for is its ability to increase one's faith. It is a reasonable argument for the existence of God. Since the general bent of the world right now is to assume that God does not exist and ridicule those who *do* believe, it provides an additional way for one to be confident in their belief in God.

The Moral Argument is Stronger Together

It is true, in a sense, that we can never convince a non-believer through argumentation that God exists. There is no one-size-fits-all argument that proves beyond a shadow of a doubt that God does, indeed, exist.[24] This is *especially* true if God is not already at work in the non-believer. However, in many, maybe even most, cases, God *is* at work. There is typically a reason someone is arguing against the existence of God. The challenge, then, is presenting an argument that is both meaningful and logical when given the opportunity. However, some arguments will work better than others. One person may find the moral argument to be utterly convincing while another thinks there is nothing of value there and would instead respond to the ontological or some other argument. Thus, the best way to argue for the existence of God is either a cumulative effect (having the space necessary to give several arguments)[25] or having a "repertoire" of individual arguments to pull from depending on the situation. In both scenarios, having multiple avenues of "attack," as it were, is only beneficial to the argument for God's existence. David Baggett and Jerry Walls put it this way, "We believe the moral argument possesses a unique appeal that may well make it the most powerful of all theistic arguments—at least for many."[26] It is worth having this argument in one's repertoire simply because for many it will be the most powerful argument for God.

---

24. Moreland, *Love Your God with All Your Mind*, 159.

25. This is the method most often used in apologetics books.

26. Baggett and Walls, *The Moral Argument*, 2.

Chapter Three

Truth

What Makes Something True?

The question of truth is quite philosophical in nature, but it is imperative to answer it in our quest to defend the faith from attacks originating both outside the Church and from within. Any post-secondary class on apologetics will include some philosophy because it is typically the world's philosophies that we are defending Christianity against. Thus, answering the age-old question "What is truth?" is at the base of many discussions surrounding Scripture; however, it is of particular importance today as the general view is that truth is relative. A typical Christian philosopher's definition of "truth" is "that which accords with reality" or something very similar.[1] This is an accurate definition, but it does not do a good job of demonstrating what this looks like exactly. Additionally, the prevailing worldview is often diametrically opposed to what the Bible says. The Bible is chock-full of truth claims and the world's response is often nearly the opposite of what Scripture says, for example:

---

1. Consider, for example, chapter two of Paul M. Gould, Travis Dickinson, and R. Keith Loftin's *Stand Firm: Apologetics and the Brilliance of the Gospel* (Nashville, TN: B&H Academics, 2018).

- The Bible says that God created everything in six days according to his design. The world says the universe came into being by random chance and that everything as we know it came through a process of minute changes over billions of years.[2]

- The Bible says that man is sinful and deserves death. The world says humans are basically good. For example, humanistic psychology assumes, "Humans are innately good, which means there is nothing inherently negative or evil about them (humans)."[3]

- The Bible says that there is "man" and "woman." The world says we can choose our own gender, and that gender is a social construct.[4]

- The Bible says that there is one God. The world says either that there is no God or that all gods are equally valid, and we cannot place one above another.[5]

As we can quickly see, the truth claims of the Bible are often flipped on their head by the world.

---

2. Robert Jastrow, *God and the Astronomers* (New York: W. W. Norton & Company, 1992), 8.

3. Saul Mcleod, "Humanistic Approach in Psychology (Humanism): Definition & Examples," *Simply Psychology*. December 20, 2023. https://www.simplypsychology.org/humanistic.html.

4. Lisa M. Diamond and Molly Butterworth, "Questioning Gender and Sexual Identity: Dynamic Links over Time," *Sex Roles*, 59 (5–6): 365–376. doi:10.1007/s11199-008-9425-3.

5. Joseph Runzo, "God, Commitment, and Other Faiths: Pluralism vs. Relativism," *Faith and Philosophy*, 5 (1988): 353–57.

Nevertheless, the answer to the question "What is truth?" is the same regardless of the topic. So, having a firm grasp of the concept of truth will be beneficial across the board. In addition to giving you a good idea of what truth is, I am going to make a massive claim and, by the end of this teaching, I hope to have proven said claim to you. Here's the claim: *Every question, every topic in this universe, and about God, has* exactly one *truth statement to it.*

I do not mean to say that a single sentence can accurately state the truth in every case. A truth statement can range anywhere from a paragraph to twenty pages long or longer in order to give an accurate statement about whatever topic or question is being discussed. Additionally, the attempt to shorten a truth claim when it needs to be longer is a dangerous endeavor that will likely result in a false or somewhat inaccurate truth statement. For example, you have likely heard the phrase "Love God, love others." Jesus' teaching on the greatest commandment is commonly summarized this way. What makes it dangerous to narrow what Jesus said down to this? It loses the *how* and *who* and the *weight* of the Old Testament. You see, Jesus was quoting the Old Testament when he said, "Love the Lord your God with all your heart and with all your soul and with all your mind and with all your strength," and "love your neighbor as yourself" (Matthew 22:37–39). Not only that though, but the situation he was in was meant to be impossible. The guy, who asked him to state the greatest commandment in the Law was essentially a lawyer of the Old Testament. He knew the Old Testament inside and out and was trying to *trap* Jesus. He anticipated Jesus saying something like "Thou shall not murder," which, though important, is not the greatest commandment. Jesus answered by summing up the *entire* Law and Prophets with the two commandments he gave.[6] By shortening what Jesus said to "Love God, love others" we lose the whole weight of the Old Testament. Additionally, we don't know *how* we are to love God and others, nor do we know *who* we are to love. Which God are we to love? Yahweh? Zeus? Ba'al? Jesus' statement tells us these things; "Love God, love others" does not.

Now that I have explained my dangerous truth statement, let's look at a few examples outside of Scripture of things that have *one* truth but may not seem like it.

Most people have seen a picture like this:

This is a pretty common example of how perspective seems to change the truth. In fact, this is exactly what the cartoonist is typically trying to get at.[7] The argument is that the number is different depending on how you look at it. But that is not how numbers work. Numbers, in every instance *except* in pictures like this, always have *one* meaning. In other words, this is *either* a "6" or a "9". It cannot be both. We determine this primarily

---

6. R. T. France, *Matthew: An Introduction and* Commentary (Downers Grove, IL: InterVarsity Press, 1985), 323.

7. I say "typically" because, in this case, I made this cartoon, and it was not my intent to demonstrate relativity.

through context. For example, if there is other writing or numbers nearby, we can ascertain the correct number by comparing it to what is around it. However, even if there is no context to tell us what number it is, it *still* has only one true number. The only way to know for sure what the number is supposed to be in a case like this is to ask the person who wrote it. *One* of these guys is correct and the other is wrong.

Another example is a half-full/half-empty glass of water. See this glass?

Would you say this glass is half full or half empty? Though this question is often used to determine if you are an optimist or a pessimist, there is actually a correct answer to this question. If you have seen *Finding Nemo* you will likely remember the scene where Marlin and Dory are in a whale's stomach. In this scene, Marlin makes a statement about how the water in the whale's mouth is already half empty. Dory counters by saying, "Hmm, I'd say it's half full." Marlin shoots back with something like, "The water's going *down*. It's half empty!" This appears to be a fun quip about the difference between an optimist and a pessimist. However, Marlin is *completely correct* in his assessment. If the last thing that happened to a cup of water is that it was filled halfway, then it is half full. If the water was poured out or drunk until it was emptied halfway, then it is half empty. When I did this illustration for a class, I filled the glass up and then left it alone. In this case, this glass was half full. I filled it up halfway and didn't touch it afterward. If I had filled it up all the way and then drunk half of it, it would have been half empty. We will come back to this example in a bit.

The final example I want to discuss is gravity. Gravity appears to be relative does it not? After all, on earth, we experience more gravity than we would on the moon and less than we would if we could stand on the surface of the sun. But, as you have probably guessed by now, gravity is not relative, at least not in the way it seems. You see, there is what is called a gravitational constant. This constant is, well, *constant*. It does not change anywhere in this universe. The *force* of gravity exerted between two objects changes based on certain factors—namely, the mass of each object and the distance between the centers of the two masses. If you know those things and the gravitational constant, then you can calculate the force of gravity anywhere in the universe. This equation is itself a truth statement about the force of gravity in the universe and looks like this when in a mathematical formula:

$$F_g = \frac{Gm_1 m_2}{r^2}$$

This concept continues in every case where there seem to be multiple truth statements. There is only one statement that is fully true even though there may appear to be multiple true statements.

What I find interesting is that this questioning of truth is not a modern invention, though it has been exasperated in modern times by relativism. So far, we have looked specifically at physical truths. That said, the same principles above apply perfectly to God and his Word. For example, in John

18:37, Jesus made a defense before Pontius Pilate saying, "You say that I am a king. For this purpose I was born and for this purpose I have come into this world—to bear witness to the truth. Everyone who is of the truth listens to my voice." To this, Pilate replied, "What is truth?" and promptly walked away from *the* authority on truth, the creator of the universe. Jesus made the claim, "I am *the* way, *the* truth, and *the* life." In fact, God and his salvation story operate on this kind of exclusivity. There isn't a myriad of ways to God, only one: belief in Jesus. There aren't hundreds or thousands of gods, there is only one. Jesus isn't *a* god; he is *the* God and the second Person of the Trinity. The list goes on and on. Thus, for a Christian, the question is not whether there *is* a single truth about each topic/question; rather it is whether we have the necessary *information* to determine what the truth statement is. Going back to the water example above, if I were not present to be able to tell someone that a given cup of water is half full, they would have a 50/50 chance of getting the answer right but would have no way of knowing if they were right. We can look for clues on the glass to try to figure it out (such as lip marks or water droplets on the side of the cup to see if it has been drunk or poured out), but we can never know *for sure* unless we are present when the drink is poured or drunk or if we are told by the person who made the drink.

Likewise, knowledge about God and his Word can come with doubt as to whether we are correct or can even know we are correct. Though I would argue that this is rarer than many make it out to be, there are legitimate examples. One major example is anything regarding end-times prophecies. We can dissect the passages that talk about the end times as much as we want and we might even come to the correct conclusions; however, we have no way of knowing *for sure* that is the correct conclusion until the end comes unless Scripture is abundantly clear. For example, the rapture is a doctrine of Scripture we can be sure will happen despite the general bent to disbelieve in it today. Plenty of Scriptural evidence supports the fact that Christians will be "caught up" to meet Jesus. That the rapture will happen is actually not up for debate. That said, the *timing* of the rapture is. I personally believe that Scripture most readily teaches a pretribulation rapture. *However*, there is potential room for a later rapture if there is a big enough distinction between the pouring out of the bowls of God's wrath which begins in Revelation 16 and the rest of the wrath found in Revelation. I do not believe that this potential is significant, but it is there. Thus, I would argue that it is best to hold to a pretribulation rapture while doing so loosely enough to not damage our faith if it does not end up happening as expected. That said, I could be wrong even though I see no truly valid argument for a time later than a pretribulation rapture. The fact is that we will not know for sure the timing of the rapture until *after* it happens. Does this mean that we should not study the end times and come to conclusions regarding it? Of course not! Scripture is clear: We are to be ready and eagerly long for Jesus' second coming.[8] We cannot be ready for it if we have no idea what to expect or what to look for. Thus, we *need* to study the signs of the times.

Different Interpretations

If my original truth statement that there is one and only one fully accurate truth statement about any given topic or question is true, why do we have so many different interpretations of Scripture? In other words, why

---

8. Wayne Grudem, *Systematic Theology: An Introduction to Biblical Doctrine* (Grand Rapids, MI: Zondervan Academic, 2020), 1344-45.

do we have so many debated doctrines in Christianity if my truth claim is accurate? All of the most hotly debated topics in Christianity such as women in ministry, old versus young earth creationism, Calvinism versus Arminianism, etc. have *one* option that is the full truth and nothing but the truth. At least, that is my claim. Many would argue that the truth of these debates and topics cannot be fully known as Scripture is not clear on said topics and that one's position comes down to how Scripture is interpreted. I would fundamentally disagree with that. But if I am correct in saying that each of these doctrines has exactly one truth statement, how can we go about determining which view is correct? To answer that question, I must first discuss two types of debates. Each of these debates fits under one of two categories. The first category is one in which Christians can relatively easily determine the correct path. In this type of debate, one side holds Scripture as supreme while the other side holds something as equal to or above Scripture. One of the most common examples of this is the old earth versus young earth debate. Only *one* side holds to the supremacy of Scripture over everything else. Every other view takes something foreign to the text of Scripture and uses it to interpret Scripture. In this case, it is contemporary science. Any version of old earth creationism involves accepting modern science as being correct. Thus, old earth creationists need to reinterpret passages of Scripture to better align with the scientific consensus. On the other hand, young earth creationism holds Scripture as supreme and interprets *scientific* findings through the lens of Scripture. This style of debate should be very easy for Christians to see the correct side. Scripture is our authority. Therefore, the side that emphasizes Scripture is likely the side that holds to the truth or is closest to it.[9]

---

9. This debate is handled in much more detail in chapters 10 and 11.

The second type of debate is when both sides have "their" Scripture verses. We see this in the Calvinism versus Arminianism debate, specifically their views on the doctrine of election. Both sides have a significant number of verses that they use to support their assertions. The problem is that both sets of verses *contradict* each other, at least when used separately. One of the most important things to know about Scripture is that it cannot contradict itself.[10] If two verses seem to contradict each other, we need to find out how they fit together in a non-contradictory way. In the case of Calvinism versus Arminianism, we see two seemingly contradictory sets of verses. On the one hand, Calvinism points out that God's sovereignty is everything.[11] He chooses who will come to him apart from any choice on the part of humans. They have many verses to back this up. On the other hand, Arminianism points out all the verses that show that humans have the ability, the free will, to choose to follow God, often to a fault.[12] Again, they have a large number of verses to support this view. The problem is that, as argued, these two ideas completely disagree with one another. Since Scripture cannot contradict itself, this simply cannot be the case. Instead, we need to look for how these sets of verses mesh together. Essentially, these verses need to meet in the middle somehow. My personal explanation for this is that God, being sovereign, has ordained the *way* to come back to him and has called all humans to turn away from their sins and follow

---

10. Due to space limitations, I am not going to defend that statement here, but the next chapter deals with this so that would be a good starting point.

11. TULIP, for example, entirely hinges on God's sovereignty. If God is sovereign in the way Calvinism points out, then TULIP is true.

12. Roger E. Olson, *Arminian Theology: Myths and Realities* (Downers Grove, IL: InterVarsity Press, 2006), 97-98.

him, but we then have the choice as to whether we will do this. This view allows for both God's sovereignty and human free will to play a distinct role in a person's salvation, which is important because, again, there are plenty of verses that support both sides of this.[13] We don't get to pick and choose which verses we will use. We need to align ourselves with what Scripture teaches. If Scripture seems to be saying something different from what we believe, even if said belief is held by millions of Christians around the world, we need to seriously examine that belief in light of Scripture. Let Scripture teach us. These types of debates often have a correct interpretation somewhere in the middle of the two opposing views which is a nuanced form of the debate.

Now that we have discussed what truth is and how there is only one truth claim for every area of life/faith, that begs the question: Does the fact that each topic has one single truth statement mean that nothing is relative? Believe it or not, there are absolutely things that are relative.[14] It might seem weird for me to say that considering I just spent significant time trying to disprove relativism. To demonstrate my point though, I would like to present you with pizza. Yes, pizza. Pizza itself has a truth claim though I am not at all sure what a fully accurate truth claim might be. That said, I will give some ideas about what might be included in a truth claim about it. A truth claim about pizza would likely define it as being a crust with a sauce of some sort, along with cheese, and sometimes other

---

13. Again, I deal with this much more extensively later, in chapter 13.

14. I don't mean "relative" in the sense of the actual definition of the term. Rather, I mean "relative" as it is meant by those who uphold moral relativism (the view that my truth is my truth and everyone else simply needs to accept it, even if it is completely unreasonable). In every case where this is true, it is a matter of personal perception and subjectivity and not actual truth.

toppings, and it's typically round in shape, and edible. These are all true things about pizza. However, whether someone *enjoys* pizza is completely relative. Not only that but what one likes on a pizza is relative as well. For example, my wife *loves* pepperoni and pineapple pizza. I, on the other hand, *hate* pineapple on my pizza. I absolutely despise it. We almost always split a pizza by ordering half with pineapple and half without pineapple. Unfortunately, an area on my side of the pizza is often contaminated pineapple juice. It's just not good. My pizza should not be *sweet or fruity*! That said, it is perfectly legitimate pizza because it fits the accepted definition of a pizza (e.g., having a crust, sauce, cheese, etc.). I cannot dispute the fact that my wife's half of the pizza is still *pizza*. I can, however, dispute whether or not it tastes any good. There are many areas of life that are similar to this and it is true even when discussing God. God is real and is as the Bible describes him, but that does not mean that a given person has to *like* that fact. The truth is the truth regardless of one's personal preferences but personal preferences are completely legitimate.

So What?

Hopefully, you have seen that there is truth and that each topic or question has a single truth statement about it. We need to hold to the truth. That is very important. If we do not have a good foundation of what truth is and we go out and engage with the culture, specifically about God, his Word, and what truth is, we are quickly going to run into problems. These can be problems in ourselves such as losing our footing because we are not firmly rooted in the truth, or they can be problems with witnessing to others. We cannot demonstrate the truth to others if we ourselves do not know or understand the truth. Additionally, we, like good investigators, need to dig and sift through the evidence and piece things together to find out what the truth is. In many, possibly even most, cases, the truth is knowable. We simply need to develop the skill of an investigator to discover these truths. Developing the skill of seeking the truth is beneficial in all areas of life, but especially when it comes to God and his Word.

Chapter Four

The Inerrancy of Scripture

The doctrine of inerrancy is an important doctrine regarding Scripture. But just how important is it? Is it an essential part of the faith? Can Christians reasonably disagree over this doctrine and still maintain an orthodox faith? These are the types of questions this chapter will address. Additionally, this chapter takes a more deductive approach to inerrancy.[1]

Brief Overview of the Debate

Before diving into the meat of the discussion, it is worthwhile to give an overview of the history of the debate on inerrancy and give an idea of just how important the debate is. While some have viewed the Bible as having errors for thousands of years, the general view of the Bible has been one of its absolute authority and infallibility.[2] The debate over inerrancy really came to a head during and after the Enlightenment when reason and

---

1. Craig Blomberg, *Can We Still Believe the Bible? An Evangelical Engagement with Contemporary Questions* (Grand Rapids, MI: Brazos Press, 2014), 122.

2. Vern S. Poythress, *Inerrancy and the Gospels: A God-Centered Approach to the Challenges of Harmonization* (Wheaton, IL: Crossway, 2012), 14.

empirical data became king rather than God's Word.[3] To be sure, while this debate has been raging for roughly the last three centuries, the idea behind the doctrine itself is not new.[4] That said, as science started to "prove" that the Bible contained errors in regard to science or history many felt the need to reduce the Bible's authority, at least in some areas, to make it agree better with what science was saying. On the flip side, many held staunchly to the fact that the Bible is *God's* Word and thus cannot reasonably contain error.[5] The latter have sought out various explanations for how portions of God's Word can be fully true yet possibly disagree with what science is teaching.

Importance of the Debate

There are few things more important than this debate. What is at stake in this debate is nothing less than God's nature.[6] That is not to say that God's nature may change based on this debate. Rather, man's understanding of his nature is what is at stake. How can we believe that God is who he says he is and does what he says he does if we believe that his very Word is full of errors? Also, how can we become more Christ-like and godly if the Bible may or may not reveal a true picture of who God and Christ are? In addition to providing an overview of what inerrancy is

---

3. Lesly F. Massey, "Biblical Inerrancy: An Anxious Reaction to Perceived Threat," *Pennsylvania Literary Journal* 13, no. 1 (Spring, 2021): 100-01, https://www.progquest.com/scholarly-journals/biblical-inerrancy-anxious-reaction-perceived-docview/2536820699/se-2.

4. John M. Frame, "Inerrancy: A Place to Live," *Journal of the Evangelical Theological Society* 57, no.1 (03, 2014): 29, https://go.openathens.net/redirector/liberty.edu?url=https://www.proquest.com/scholarly-journals/inerrancy-place-live/docview/1534298360/se-2.

5. Keith L. Johnson, *Theology as Discipleship* (Downers Grove, IL: InterVarsity Press, 2015), 77.

6. For a good overview of the importance of inerrancy see *Vital Issues in the Inerrancy Debate*, edited by F. David Farnell, Norman L. Geisler, Joseph M. Holden, William C. Roach, and Phil Fernandes (Eugene, OR: Wipf &Stock Publishers, 2015), 20-23.

and how it is similar or different to infallibility, this chapter will argue that not only is the doctrine of the inerrancy of Scripture true, but it is also necessary for Christians to hold to in order to avoid apostasy.

Overview of the Terms "Inerrancy" and "Infallibility"

Inerrancy and infallibility may seem to be the same terms or even may seem to be unnecessary terms to some people. To be sure, these *are* theological terms for something that could be explained another way; however, they are good terms for describing the Bible. Additionally, we cannot truly address the inerrancy of Scripture unless we first understand the similarities and differences between these words.

Infallibility

Infallibility is the first term to be looked at as it is the earlier term of the two. Before "inerrancy" began being used, "infallibility" was the term of choice for theologians.

What Is Infallibility?

Infallibility is an interesting word. From a base meaning of something not being fallible or able to fail, it seems to be essentially the same word as inerrant (without error).[7] This is precisely how it used to be used. Infallibility used to be used to say that all of God's Word cannot fail. However, as attacks on inerrancy have happened, it has changed a bit depending on who is using the word. For some, like me, infallibility and inerrancy remain interchangeable terms, though with a slight nuance which will be addressed fully later. That said, right now the main thing to know

---

7. Daniel J. Treier and Walter A. Elwell, eds, *Evangelical Dictionary of Theology* (Grand Rapids, MI: Baker Academic, 2017), 791.

is that infallibility deals with *possibility*. Specifically, if Scripture is to be called "infallible" it cannot have the *possibility* of failing, otherwise it is not infallible. This is based on a simple definition of the word itself without theological nuance being added in.

Is It Sufficient on Its Own?

The answer to this question is, unfortunately, an unsatisfying "yes and no" because it depends entirely on what a person means when they say God's Word is infallible. To make matters worse, this can be very challenging to determine. For example, I have had several conversations with Mormons. I often found these conversations to be thoroughly frustrating because the same words would be used to describe two totally different things. When a Mormon talks about "Jesus" they are not talking about the same Jesus that I am talking about. This results in a lot of talking past one another. Similarly, when some people use infallible/infallibility on their own to describe Scripture, they mean precisely what the basic meaning of the word is. In this case, yes, infallibility is sufficient by itself as it has the same basic meaning as inerrant. Others, when they talk about infallibility, do so with a different definition or idea about what infallibility is or what it applies to. In these cases, it is almost always *insufficient* because these others add in qualifiers that allow much of Scripture to be considered fallible in some regard.

Inerrancy

Inerrancy, the second word to be addressed, is necessary to engage with for a couple of reasons. First, it is technically the subject of this chapter. Second it is also the term that is most highly debated between the two. Many churches, organizations, and Christians uphold "infallibility" while simultaneously rejecting "inerrancy."

What Is Inerrancy?

Inerrancy, as already mentioned, is having no errors. To say that God's Word is inerrant is to say that, in its original manuscripts, it has no errors and is fully truthful in all that it claims.[8] However, in the same way that infallibility is sometimes used in ways outside of its basic meaning, inerrancy can also mean different things based on who is using it.[9] These differences will be looked at more in the next major section of this chapter.

How Inerrancy and Infallibility Interact

There is a nuanced difference between infallibility and inerrancy. As shown above, infallibility has to do with whether something *can* fail. Inerrancy, on the other hand, deals with whether something *did* fail. This nuance is significant even though it may not appear so. Take this book for example. It is entirely possible, however unlikely, that this book is free of all errors and is fully truthful in all its claims. Thus, while it is doubtful, this document can legitimately be *inerrant*. That said, it can never be infallible. This is because I, being the author of the book, am not infallible. Thus, even if the book itself is inerrant, it is *not* infallible as there is the *possibility*, based on the author, that it can fail. In the case of Scripture, inerrancy is the natural outpouring of God's infallibility. God *is* infallible. He cannot err. Therefore, his Word is likewise infallible and thus inerrant.

---

8. Gregg R. Allison, *The Baker Compact Dictionary of Theological Terms* (Grand Rapids, MI: Baker Books, 2016), 79.

9. Millard Erikson, *Christian Theology* (Grand Rapids, MI: Baker Academic, 2013), 191.

Overview of the Major Different Views on Inerrancy

There are a number of views on "inerrancy" that must be defined. No inerrancy, limited inerrancy, and total inerrancy are the ones we will look at, though there are others.

No Inerrancy

This is a simple one. Basically, those who hold the view of "no inerrancy" do not believe that the Bible is inerrant at all.[10] This typically comes in the form of looking only at the human authors of Scripture and noting, correctly, that all humans are fallible and make errors. However, the Bible is not merely a creation by man despite what the historical-critical method of interpreting Scripture might try to suggest.[11]

Sometimes those who hold to no inerrancy simply say that it is an irrelevant doctrine. The main argument here is that this doctrine distracts from what actually matters.[12] Some even go so far as to declare the doctrine of inerrancy as the "worst heresy that has ever afflicted the Church, and it is an evil from which the Church must repent."[13] This last one is admittedly an extreme view, but it does fit under the no inerrancy category.

---

10. Wynne Carlton, "Inerrancy is Not Enough: A Lesson in Epistemology from Clark Pinnock on Scripture," *Unio cum Christo* 2, no. 2 (October 2016): 68. This is also an interesting look into someone who once held to inerrancy but later rejected it.

11. See, for example, 1 Peter 1:20-21.

12. R. Albert Mohler, et al., *Five Views on Biblical Inerrancy*, eds. J. Merrick and Stephen M. Garrett (Grand Rapids, MI: Zondervan, 2013), 146.

13. Rodger L. Cragun, *The Ultimate Heresy: The Doctrine of Biblical Inerrancy* (Eugene, OR: Wipf & Stock Publishers, 2018), xviii.

Limited Inerrancy

Unlike the no inerrancy camp, the limited inerrancy camp is more difficult to discuss succinctly. From a very broad perspective, it means what it means—some of the Bible is inerrant and some of it is not. However, what exactly someone who holds to limited inerrancy believes about what is inerrant and what is not is not as simple of a question. For example, some would say that it is only inerrant in areas of faith and practice but is not in all other areas, such as scientific or historical claims.[14] Regardless of the precise view, the main takeaway is that limited inerrantists *limit* inerrancy in some way. As will be discussed in a later section, the limited inerrancy position has a distinct problem in that its proponents need to apply something foreign to the text of Scripture in order to determine what counts as "inerrant."

Total Inerrancy

True total inerrancy is best exemplified by the "Chicago Statement on Biblical Inerrancy."[15] This large statement on inerrancy basically states that Scripture is without error in the original documents and is fully truthful regarding everything it says. Since this is an absolute statement, adherents of total inerrancy need to explain exactly what this means. Does this mean that the original documents had perfect grammar? Does it mean that the Bible can never record a lie? Does the Bible need to be scientifically precise as science is viewed today? Total inerrantists need to have answers to these, and similar, questions. That said, pick up a book on inerrancy or systematic theology and you will almost always find a robust defense of

---

14. Grudem, *Systematic Theology*, 88.

15. "The Chicago Statement on Biblical Inerrancy," *Evangelical Review of Theology*, 4, no.1 (1980).

what total inerrancy actually entails. Total inerrancy has also been divided into multiple levels, namely absolute inerrancy and full inerrancy.[16] The difference is that an absolute inerrantist views Scripture as being fully scientifically accurate and thus must be able to explain any apparent discrepancies while a full inerrantist would argue that many of these things are just how they appear to the human eye rather than being scientifically based facts.[17] One important thing to remember is that genre plays a distinct role in this. The Bible has different genres that need to be taken into account in some way. On this, Kevin Vanhoozer says, "Two biblical passages may not be inerrant in exactly the same way; that is, not every biblical statement must state historical truth. Inerrancy must be construed broadly enough to encompass the truth expressed in Scripture's poetry, romances, proverbs, parables, as well as histories."[18] While I may not like how this is phrased exactly, it does point out an important part of the Bible and a challenge that needs to be kept in mind as one seeks to interpret Scripture. Vanhoozer brings up yet another consideration of the total inerrancy view when he states, "The Bible's witness to its subject matter is always true; the interpreter's witness to the text, by contrast, suffers from various forms of existential short-sightedness, confessional tunnel vision,

---

16. Erikson, *Christian Theology*, 191.

17. Ibid. See Erikson's molten pool example.

18. Kevin J. Vanhoozer, "The Semantics of Biblical Literature: Truth and Scripture's Diverse Literary Forms," in D.A. Carson adn John D. Woodbridge (eds.), *Hermeneutics, Authority, and Canon* (Leicester: IVP, 1986): 86.

and cultural myopia."[19] Just because God's Word is inerrant does not mean that our interpretation of it is.

The Claims Scripture Makes About God and Itself *Require* Either a Total Rejection or Total Acceptance of Its Authority

Anakin Skywalker, when he first became Darth Vader, told Obi-Wan Kenobi, "If you're not with me, then you're my enemy!" Scripture does the same. It claims certain things that force either a total acceptance of its authority or a total rejection of the same.

What Does Scripture Say About God?

Scripture makes some very significant claims about the nature of God. For one, it commonly argues, or shows God arguing, that every word from his mouth is true and perfect. Psalm 12:6 says, "The words of Yahweh are pure words, like silver refined in a furnace on the ground, purified seven times." Basically, the words of Yahweh are perfectly pure. Similarly, Proverbs 30:5 says, "Every word of God proves true; he is a shield to those who take refuge in him." God cannot tell a lie as every word that he speaks is true. On the idea that God cannot lie, Numbers 23:19 says, "God is not a man, that he should lie, or a son of man, that he should change his mind. Has he not said, and will he not do it? Or has he spoken, and will he not fulfill it?" Hebrews 6:18 argues that it is *impossible* for God to lie.

---

19. Kevin J. Vanhoozer, "Lost in Interpretation? Truth, Scripture, and Hermeneutics," *Journal of the Evangelical Theological Society* 48, no. 1 (March 2005): 97, https://go.openathens.net/redirector/liberty.edu?url=https://www.proquest.com/scholarly-journals/lost-interpretation-truth-scripture-hermeneutics1/docview/211221919/se-2.

Another significant claim that Scripture makes about God is that he is unchanging. One such example comes from God's own mouth. Malachi 3:6 says, "For I, Yahweh, do not change; therefore you, O sons of Jacob, are not consumed." Other examples of God's unchangeability can be seen in Psalm 102:27, Hebrews 13:8, James 1:17, etc.

God cannot lie, he is unchanging, and his words are perfect according to Scripture. This is some fantastic and profound truth but this alone does not prove anything. Thus, we need to look at what Scripture says about itself. Is it God's Word?

What Does Scripture Say About Itself?

Scripture makes significant claims about God, but what does it say about itself? For one, it claims to be *from* God. One of the most recognizable references to what Scripture says about itself is found in 2 Timothy 3:16 which says, "All Scripture is breathed out by God and profitable for teaching, for reproof, for correction, and for training in righteousness." Declaring that *all Scripture* is God-breathed clearly states the origin of Scripture; however, some have raised objections to this. For example, an important hermeneutical consideration about this verse is that it was likely referring to the Old Testament. Some argue then that it does not include the New Testament. That said, Peter said that Paul's writing was Scripture just like the Old Testament. He said, "Just as our beloved brother Paul also wrote to you according to the wisdom given him, as he does in all his letters when he speaks in them of these matters. There are some things in them that are hard to understand, which the ignorant and unstable twist to their own destruction, *as they do the other Scriptures*" (2 Peter 3:15–16, emphasis added). Thus, it is best to consider Paul's statement that all Scripture is God-breathed to include the New Testament.

Another important reference to what the Bible says regarding itself is found in 2 Peter 1:20–21 which says, "Knowing this first of all, that no prophecy of Scripture comes from someone's own interpretation. For no prophecy was ever produced by the will of man, but men spoke from God as they were carried along by the Holy Spirit." This passage says that every prophecy is from God rather than man, but that just refers to prophecies about the future, right? Not so. "Prophecy" refers to a couple of different things. It is both *foretelling* and *forthtelling* the mind or will of God. One has to do with the future while the other has to do with teaching and doing God's will in the present. All of Scripture fits under this. God is revealing himself through the writers of Scripture. A prophet tells the people what God wants them to know whether that is future-focused or present-focused.

Finally, Hebrews 4:12 says, "For the word of God is living and active, sharper than any two-edged sword, piercing to the division of soul and of spirit, of joints and of marrow, and discerning the thoughts and intentions of the heart". It is impossible for any book except a book that is from God to be considered "living and active." Additionally, the writer of Hebrews is connecting this to the fact that God is the *living God* (Hebrews 3:12). Just like God is the living God, so too is his Word living and active. God proclaims, "So shall my word be that goes out from my mouth; it shall not return to me empty, but it shall accomplish that which I purpose, and shall succeed in the thing for which I sent it" (Isaiah 55:11). These Old and New Testament verses both talk about God's Word in a way that demonstrates that it is more than just human writing that is static and unable to do anything. It is living and active like God is living and active.

While there are many other verses that can be discussed regarding this, these are sufficient to demonstrate that the Bible declares that all of Scripture is from God rather than man.

Before moving on, it is important to ask: Why is it not circular reasoning to use the Bible to defend the Bible? It is not circular reasoning because of the nature of God's Word. If God really did inspire the Bible and it is indeed without error and does not contradict itself just as God cannot contradict himself, then everything in the Bible would be in accord with the truth. This is not the case with any other book in history. Every other book, being written by fallible humans and fallible humans alone, cannot make the same claims. It *is* circular reasoning to use any other book to interpret itself as I am doing with Scripture, but it is *not* circular reasoning with the Bible.

Scripture Is Either God's Word or It Is Not

Based on what Scripture says about itself and God, it must either be a false and unreliable witness or inerrant and infallible. This is because Scripture makes the claim that it is from God inspiring the writers, with much of Scripture being claimed to have been *directly* spoken by God (with the common "thus says Yahweh" phrase). If these scriptural claims are true, then it is without a doubt God's Word. Since God cannot lie and every word from his mouth is true then God's Word, the Old and New Testaments, must necessarily be inerrant and infallible. This is simply because God himself is without error and incapable of failing. Flip it over and the same is true. If Scripture errs, it is not God's Word because he cannot fail, nor can his words err.

The Doctrine of the Inerrancy of Scripture Is Necessary to Avoid Apostasy

Some suggest that the inerrancy of Scripture is unnecessary or even heretical; however, below I will demonstrate that it is *necessary* to hold firmly to it if we wish to avoid falling in our faith.

Not Holding to Inerrancy Makes Every Doctrine in Scripture Suspect

One of the major arguments in Stephen Andrew's article on biblical inerrancy is the epistemological argument. He states, "The argument holds that, once inerrancy is surrendered, all of Scripture becomes suspect in regards to trustworthiness."[20] Basically, if Scripture is not fully inerrant, then *every* part must be viewed as untrustworthy until it has been proven trustworthy. But who, or what, is the arbiter of truth in this case? In every instance, the arbiter of truth is *not* God's Word. Something else must be applied to Scripture to combat this. For example, the biblical account of creation has to be interpreted through the lens of science rather than the other way around. Many adherents of limited inerrancy are aware of this exact problem. However, the solution is often to elevate their own minds, their reason, as being the arbiter of truth on whether specific passages are inerrant.[21] Obviously, there is a distinct danger here. If one's mind or reason determines whether a passage is inerrant, then it is only a matter of time until relativism rears its ugly head, and personal beliefs begin to twist

---

20. Stephen L. Andrew, "Biblical Inerrancy," *Chafer Theological Seminary Journal* 8.1 (Winter 2002): 10.

21. Andrew, "Biblical Inerrancy," 17.

Scripture in ways it was never meant to be twisted. This leads directly to the next argument.

The "Slippery Slope" Argument

The slippery slope argument is essentially that, once the inerrancy of Scripture is rejected, the person, group of people, or organization that rejected it would slip away from orthodoxy. The logic is simple. If God's Word is not held as inerrant and infallible by the person studying it then they are liable to twist Scripture to their own agendas rather than let Scripture teach them. Some insist that the slippery slope argument needs not to be used because it is not guaranteed. For example, Stephen Andrew points out that Fuller Theological Seminary removed "inerrancy" from their statement of faith roughly seventy years ago and has not since slipped into unorthodoxy.[22] Unfortunately, this is a lack of understanding of what constitutes "falling from orthodoxy." While Fuller has not made any additional changes to their statement of faith, they *have* demonstrated significant breaches in orthodoxy. This can readily be seen in some of the classes offered, the professors and their teachings, and how these things have affected churches.[23] On one occasion, this resulted in a backlash prompting Fuller to remove a class from their registry only to reinstate it a year later with less emphasis on it.[24] It is clear that, even when the

---

22. Ibid., 10.

23. For example, C. Peter Wagner taught for approximately 30 years at Fuller while his teachings both there and outside of Fuller have had a massive impact and much of that is outside of orthodoxy. Additionally, I have personally seen a church descend into unorthodoxy based on the teachings of other Fuller professors.

24. Alister McGrath, *Christianity's Dangerous Idea: The Protestant Revolution—A History from the Sixteenth Century to the Twenty-First* (New York, NY: HarperCollins Publishers, 2007), 419.

"official" stance of a group or organization is still in line with orthodoxy (sans inerrancy), the slippery slope is a real thing that needs to be argued in the case of someone rejecting inerrancy.

Conclusion

The doctrine of the inerrancy of Scripture is an extremely important topic. Satan and the world want nothing more than for Christians to water down the truth in God's Word to the point where entire sections of Scripture are rejected as being myth or merely culturally subjective. The crazy thing is that it is not even the world that is the main threat here. It is fellow believers in Christ. Yet, it is not that crazy. Scripture is clear that the biggest threats to true faith are those who come from within as wolves in sheep's clothing and well-meaning but misguided believers. A high view of the doctrine of inerrancy is necessary to combat many of the attacks that have come against Scripture and the church in modern times.[25] Part of this is recognizing that total inerrancy is the view that most accurately aligns with God and his Word. God does not lie, nor does he change. Every word from his mouth is true and the Bible is *his* Word. This needs to be held to staunchly, otherwise, we are liable to fall into unorthodoxy.[26]

---

25. Gregory K. Beale, *The Erosion of Inerrancy in Evangelicalism: Responding to New Challenges to Biblical Authority* (Wheaton, IL: Crossway Books, 2008), 17. Beale gives two possibilities as to why inerrancy is being eroded in evangelical circles.

26. John MacArthur, ed., *The Inerrant Word: Biblical, Historical, Theological, and Pastoral Perspectives* (Wheaton, IL: Crossway, 2016), 1.

Chapter Five

Gnosticism: A Biblical and Historical Response

We can see from the earliest texts of Christianity, namely the Epistles, that different interpretations and understandings of who Jesus is and how we should live the Christian life have been around since the beginning.[1] Most of the Epistles were written at least partly to address some form of false teaching or false practice. One of these early forms of false teaching was Gnosticism. Gnosticism seemed to spring up at the same time as Christianity did. On the one hand, it happened so quickly that it likely could not be rooted in Christianity itself, but on the other hand, it quickly latched onto much of what was taught in the Bible and interpreted it for its own gain. But what even is Gnosticism, and is it heretical? How did it come to fruition so quickly and what was the response by the apostles and the early church? This chapter will give an overview of the rise of the movement of Gnosticism in the early church and discuss the orthodox responses to this heresy by both the church father Irenaeus and the apostles which show that Gnosticism is, indeed, heretical.

---

1. John Behr, *Irenaeus of Lyons: Identifying Christianity* (Oxford: Oxford University Press, 2013), 7.

The Rise of Gnosticism and Its Teachings

Before engaging with Gnosticism itself, I find it worthwhile to address why I am including this teaching in this book. Many might suggest that this is merely academic in the sense that Gnosticism was an *old* problem that the church dealt with and thus it does not have any real bearing for us today. This could not be further from the truth. Gnosticism never fully died out. Flavors of it have continued to exist throughout the centuries. Additionally, with the discovery of the many Gnostic texts at Nag Hammadi, it has regained influence. Certain theologians treat these texts as of equal value to the church as the orthodox writings and even Scripture itself. In many ways, Gnosticism has combined with Eastern religion to produce a syncretistic religion that has begun to make its way into Christianity in the form of New Age Mysticism. Christians who are not diligent in "testing the spirits" (1 John 4:1) often find themselves sucked into these teachings. Overall, this teaching is *vastly* important for the modern church to understand and deal with.

What is Gnosticism?

The term "Gnosticism" comes from the Greek word γνῶσις meaning "knowledge." In particular, the Gnostic movement claims to have special or exclusive knowledge, which is why they received the term to describe the movement, despite never using it of themselves. There is evidence of its influence within Christianity from an early time but it became a major factor in the second century as evidenced by the orthodox responses to it and the many Gnostic texts that were discovered last century in Egypt some of which date back to the second century.

Major Beliefs

One of the major beliefs in Gnosticism is the idea that flesh is bad/evil while the spirit is good. As such, a common theme in Gnosticism is that Jesus did not actually come in the flesh. He only *appeared* to come in the flesh since if he had actually come in the flesh he would be corrupted like the rest of the cosmos. Nothing material can be saved.[2] Another major view is that one must obtain "secret knowledge" in order to gain eternal life. This idea is at the beginning of the Gospel of Thomas, for example.[3] Additionally, it is generally a very syncretistic movement. It pulls from many different sources to develop its teachings.

An Actual Religion or a Collection of Similar Teachings?

The use of the term "Gnosticism" makes it seem as though there is one religion or one heretical movement called "Gnosticism." However, this does not really do the term justice. Although Gnostics tend to have specific shared beliefs, they are really a rather diverse group.[4] Especially when considering the more modern flavors of Gnosticism, many different beliefs seem to fit under the umbrella of Gnosticism, similar to how many modern church denominations share core beliefs yet have distinct differences between them. Thus, it can, and probably should, be argued that Gnosticism is an actual religion but there is diversity within it. Otherwise, it poses challenges to using an umbrella term like "Christian" for all of the different denominations. Since most would claim that different

---

2. Robert M. Grant, *Irenaeus of Lyons*. (London: Routledge, 1996), 48.

3. Bart D. Ehrman, *Lost Scriptures: Books That Did Not Make It into the New Testament* (Oxford: Oxford University Press, 2003), 19.

4. Eduard Iricinschi, et al., *Beyond the Gnostic Gospels: Studies Building on the Work of Elaine Pagels* (Tübingen: Mohr Siebeck, 2013), 62.

denominations are still "Christian" then it would be reasonable to apply this concept to Gnosticism as well.

Gnosticism's Roots Prior to Christianity

Gnosticism is not rooted in Christianity. The core concepts, while Christian adjacent, are not actually Christian. To be sure, Christianity provided an excellent area for the growth of Gnosticism but it did not *start* there. Though there are other influences, Greek philosophy is one of the major players in the development of Gnosticism.[5]

Greek Philosophy's Influence

In his defense against the Valentinians, Irenaeus states that they pulled from the poets and philosophers and merely renamed the things that were said.[6] This is definitely true. There is much similarity between the dualistic spirit versus material ideas of Greek philosophy.[7] The fact that Irenaeus latched onto this is further evidence that Greek philosophy had a significant impact on Gnosticism. It would also help to make sense of the fast rise of Gnosticism in Christianity. The ideas were already there, they just needed to have the New Testament to coalesce into a more formal movement.

Gnosticism as a Christian Offshoot

While Gnosticism clearly has roots outside of Christianity, it also seems to at least be heavily influenced by it. Specifically, the apostle Paul

---

5. Greek philosophy is the only influence that will be addressed here; however, for someone interested in a deeper dive, I would recommend looking into its Eastern religion and Jewish roots in addition to the Greek influences.

6. Grant, *Irenaeus of Lyons*, 83.

7. Stephen J. Patterson, James M. Robinson, and Hans-Gebhard Bethge, *The Fifth Gospel: The Gospel of Thomas Comes of Age* (London: T & T Clark, 2011), 48.

appears to have been a key influence for many of the early Gnostics and Irenaeus viewed Gnosticism as being a *Christian* heresy. In other words, Gnosticism may have had roots outside of Christianity, but it latched onto Christianity and the most prolific writer of the New Testament so closely that early church fathers viewed it as a heretical offshoot of Christianity.

The Apostle Paul's Influence on Gnosticism

Despite Paul's rejection of Gnosticism, the early Gnostics (and, indeed, even modern ones) viewed Paul as somewhat of a champion of their faith. In response to a commenter who stated that 1 Corinthians 15 is the culmination of an anti-Gnostic polemic, religion historian Elaine Pagels said that if this is true then the Gnostic interpretation of the passage is "nothing less than astonishing" because "not only do gnostic exegetes fail to grasp the whole point of Paul's writings, but they even claim his letters as a primary source of their own gnostic theology."[8] First Corinthians 15 in particular seems to have been thoroughly interpreted by the early Gnostics as demonstrating that Paul himself was "initiated" as a Gnostic and was teaching Gnostic views. Modern Gnostics and mystics still view Paul in the highest regard as being the first of the Gnostic teachers. That said, it is obvious that both modern and ancient Gnostics interpret Paul through a lens that is foreign to the plain reading of the text. They add in their own theology and desires which has allowed them to twist Paul's words into something that they were never meant to be. This very well may be part of what Peter was warning about in 2 Peter 3:16 when he said, "There are

---

8. Elaine H. Pagels, "'The Mystery of the Resurrection': A Gnostic Reading of 1 Corinthians 15," *Journal of Biblical Literature* 93, no. 2 (1974): 276. https://doi.org/10.2307/3263097. This article, as a whole, argues quite firmly for how thoroughly the Gnostics had championed that Paul was a Gnostic and that his teaching was compatible with the Gnostic view.

some things in them [Paul's letters] that are hard to understand, which the ignorant and unstable twist to their own destruction, as they do the other Scriptures." Paul does indeed write many difficult things, but the Gnostic use of Paul's writing is clearly twisting what he says even if 2 Peter 3:16 is not a reference to this Gnostic tendency.

Irenaeus's View that Gnosticism Was a Christian Heresy

Irenaeus demonstrates, quite clearly, that the early Gnostics desired to meld the Scriptures with their own twisted teachings about knowledge and mysteries. He points to a bunch of verses that are commonly taken from the Bible and then twisted outside of what may be considered normal exegesis.[9] He also shows how Ptolemaeus interprets the first chapter of John as clearly teaching the first Ogdoad.

The Apostolic Response

The apostles' epistles are the earliest known responses to the rise of Gnosticism, at least in written form. Gnosticism was likely argued against in person and amongst church congregants even before the epistles were written, but the earliest evidence we have comes in the form of the epistles. This, coupled with the fact that the epistles are Scripture, indicates the importance of seeing what the apostles have to say regarding this problem.

Paul

It has been discussed that Paul was seen as one of the apostles, if not *the* apostle, for the Gnostics; however, Paul argues against the Gnostic view

---

9. Grant, *Irenaeus of Lyons*, 50-52.

directly at least once.[10] Additionally, there are other passages that may be Pauline responses to Gnosticism.

1 Timothy

"O Timothy, guard the deposit entrusted to you. Avoid the irreverent babble and contradictions of what is falsely called 'knowledge,' for by professing it some have swerved from the faith" (1 Timothy 6:20–21). This focus on that which is "falsely called knowledge" is almost certainly a reference to early forms of Gnosticism rearing its ugly head. That said, this exhortation to Timothy goes beyond just the Gnostics. In his commentary on this verse, Donald Guthrie notes that this reference to "knowledge" is not limited to the early Gnostics. He says, "It is evident in all modern cults which claim an exclusive grasp of true knowledge."[11] While that is absolutely true, it is a good thing to remember that the original argument was against Gnostic ideas especially considering how Gnosticism has gained more traction in recent years.

First Timothy 6:20–21 very clearly lays out an argument against false "knowledge," however, it is not the only reference in 1 Timothy to Gnostic teachings. Specifically, 1 Timothy 3:16 explicitly states that Jesus came in the flesh. Gnostics cannot teach that Jesus came in the flesh for flesh is material and material cannot be good or saved. Additionally, 1 Timothy 4:1–5 says that many will depart the faith by "devoting themselves to deceitful spirits and teachings of demons" that forbid marriage and prescribe abstinence from foods that God created. Since Gnosticism believes that

---

10. Stanley E. Porter and David I. Yoon, *Paul and Gnosis* (Leiden, Netherlands: Brill, 2016) 107.

11. Donald Guthrie, *The Pastoral Epistles: An Introduction and Commentary* (Downers Grove, IL: InterVarsity Press, 1990) 133.

there is nothing material that is good or can be saved, this is an argument against Gnosticism and similar heresies.

Other Possible Responses

Some argue that Paul is arguing against Gnosticism in 1 Corinthians, and in a sense he is. This epistle argues against many of the teachings of the Gnostics without specifically targeting Gnostics. For example, in 1 Corinthians 2:2 Paul says he only preached Christ crucified. This is not necessarily against Gnosticism in the sense that it was directed at it. It *could* have been, but it also could have just been Paul explaining himself and the gospel. Another possible reference to Gnosticism is in Colossians 2:18–23.

John

The Johannine epistles have a couple of references against Gnostic ideas. Additionally, some claim that John's Gospel is a direct response to the Gospel of Thomas. Both of these areas will be addressed in this section.

Arguments Against Gnostic Ideas in John's Epistles

There are a couple of places in John's epistles where he argues against some of the ideas that the Gnostics shared. While there are other possibilities, only the following verses will be examined: 1 John 4:2–3a and 2 John 1:7.

First John 4:2–3a says, "By this you know the Spirit of God: every spirit that confesses that Jesus Christ has come in the flesh is from God, and every spirit that does not confess Jesus is not from God." One of the major beliefs in Gnosticism is the idea that Jesus, or at least the Christ, could not have come in the flesh. John says that anyone, any spirit, who does not confess that Jesus Christ came in the flesh is not from God.

Similarly, 2 John 1:7 says, "For many deceivers have gone out into the world, those who do not confess the coming of Jesus Christ in the flesh.

Such a one is the deceiver and the antichrist." Again, Jesus Christ coming in the flesh is antithetical to anything that Gnosticism teaches.

Did John Write His Gospel in Response to the Gospel of Thomas?

Ever since the Gospel of Thomas was discovered, there have been people who have argued that John's Gospel was a direct, orthodox response to it. But is there any validity to this? It is doubtful. First off, one of the common things that is argued is that the apostle Thomas is shown as not believing Jesus is who he says he is until he feels Jesus' wounds and sees that they are real flesh. Thus, John was almost sarcastically pointing out how Thomas needed to feel the material Jesus and is thus proof that Gnosticism is wrong. That said, "doubting" Thomas as he is commonly called is unlikely to have been the author of the Gospel of Thomas (or the one that it is attributed to anyway).[12] Additionally, the Gospel of John likely predates the Gospel of Thomas by a fair amount. There *are* many things in the Gospel of John that argue against Gnostic teachings but they are likely to be more similar to 1 Corinthians in the sense that they are stating facts about Jesus rather than arguing against the Gospel of Thomas or similar writings.

Irenaeus of Lyons Response

Irenaeus of Lyons was a second-century theologian and bishop who was a former student of Polycarp, who was said to have been a student of the apostle John.[13] His defense against the early form of Gnosticism was the

---

12. Patterson, *The Fifth Gospel*, 30-31.

13. C. Douglas Weaver, and Rady Roldán-Figueroa, *Exploring Christian Heritage: A Reader in History and Theology* (Waco, TX: Baylor University Press, 2017), 17.

first though by no means the last. As he was the first major defender of what has since been considered the orthodox faith, his life and work are quite important, especially since the discoveries of many of the Gnostic texts in 1945.[14] These are the very texts or types of texts that house the kinds of teachings that Irenaeus argued against in his work *The Refutation and Overthrowal of Knowledge Falsely So-Called* which is commonly referred to as *Against Heresies*. Some have taken these texts as evidence that there were legitimate Christian interpretations outside of what has been considered orthodox.[15] While there were indeed different interpretations, they were not all "legitimate," as can clearly be seen in the apostle's writing above, and it is also thoroughly refuted by Irenaeus as will be seen below.

Irenaeus begins his work by saying, "Some persons reject the truth and introduce false statements and 'endless genealogies, which provide questions,' as the Apostle says, 'rather than the divine training that is in faith.'"[16] He goes on to say that, on the pretext of "knowledge," they overthrow people who are unable to tell the difference between what is true and what is false. Thus, he connects the claims of "knowledge" that his opponents had with what Paul was saying in 1 Timothy 6:20–21. He argues that false teaching can look even more real than the real thing unless someone has the ability to test it and prove it to be fraudulent. Additionally, in his preface, Irenaeus makes no claim to be a good writer or skilled in rhetoric. Instead, he writes with simplicity and love so that his readers may understand and further develop the ideas he presents.

---

14. Patterson, *The Fifth Gospel*, 27.

15. Behr, *Irenaeus of Lyons*, 2.

16. Grant, *Irenaeus of Lyons*, 43. Irenaeus is quoting 1 Timothy 1:4.

Against the Valentinians

The Valentinians were one of the main sects of Gnosticism that was around in Irenaeus's time. In his preface to his first two books, Irenaeus says, "Therefore, after reading the commentaries of those who call themselves disciples of Valentinus, and meeting some of them and having fully understood their teaching, I considered it necessary to show you, beloved, their portentous and profound mysteries, which 'not all understand' [Matt. 19:11], because not all have lost their brains!"[17] He gives the reason for his writing as setting forth their teaching plainly so that it can be refuted as "absurd, inconsistent, and discordant with the truth." Book 1 then has Irenaeus delve into the depths of what the Valentinians believe. It truly is a dizzying array of ideas that have no basis in Scripture except "the scriptures which they have been able to adapt and assimilate to their fiction."[18] These Scriptures are twisted beyond recognition. Also, how the Valentinians viewed God and the creation of the world is much more in line with other religions that have pantheons of gods who, through their interactions, produced offspring and the material world.[19] Irenaeus even goes so far as to make an argument for the creation of different types of water in accord with the ways in which the Valentinians might.[20] It does a good job of showing how foolish their views are, but Irenaeus says, "'Fruits' of this kind are entirely suited to their argument."[21] It is possible to go

---

17. Ibid., 43.

18. Ibid., 46.

19. Ibid., 83.

20. Ibid., 48.

21. Ibid.

on and on about the "mysteries" of the Valentinians, but that is not the purpose of this section.

One of Irenaeus's convincing defenses actually comes in the form of laying out the tradition received by the apostles, saying, "For if the languages in the world are dissimilar, the power of the tradition is one and the same."[22] This is the tradition that comes from a plain reading of the Scriptures rather than seeking some "hidden" knowledge supposedly found in the Scriptures. Furthermore, he argues that, unlike the whole church which has "one and the same faith in all the world," the Valentinians, when they come together, "not only do not make the same statements about the same things but give contradictory answers in content and expression alike."[23] Essentially, they have no true unity in their beliefs, nor can they as they are not firmly rooted in Scripture. Rather, their religion is rooted in fiction as is evidenced by their creation of words to name things in ways that no one else ever has. Irenaeus expounds on this idea with a parody by showing that nothing prevents someone from taking the same subject and giving their own names for it. He does so, quite humorously, by giving fruit names to the same things the Valentinians were talking about. In general, Irenaeus argues effectively and convincingly against the views of the Valentinians by using both his own logic and Scripture.

Against Marcion

Marcion believed that the supposed differences between the Old Testament God and the God of Christ were incompatible. He believed the God of the Old Testament to be evil and judgmental while the God of

---

22. Ibid., 54.

23. Ibid., 55.

Christ was good. Irenaeus argues against this view.[24] He argued that God must be both good and judgmental in order to *be* God. If God is not both then he, quite simply, is not God. Irenaeus even goes so far as to say that Plato "appears to be more religious than they are, for he acknowledged the one God who is both just and good, has power over all, and himself performs judgment."[25] Interestingly, he talks about how he loves them (those who teach this false view) even more than they think they love themselves. Should they accept the true love from Irenaeus, it would save them as it is "like a harsh medicine that eats away the foreign and superfluous flesh formed on a wound."[26] Many modern Christians struggle with the same thing that Marcion did. They view the Old Testament God and the New Testament God as different. Thus, though they are nearly two thousand years old, Irenaeus's words against this false teaching still ring true to this day in a very practical way. God must be both good and just in order to be God.

Conclusion

Though Gnosticism has roots that extend past the beginning of Christianity, it became a more formal, though heretical, movement after the establishment of Christianity. Gnostics seemed to have a high regard for the apostle Paul in particular, but many of their beliefs run directly counter to Scripture including Paul's own writings. Irenaeus of Lyons argued against their views effectively as did Paul and John in their epistles. This is impor-

---

24. Ibid., 107.

25. Ibid.

26. Ibid., 108.

tant for us to know as modern Christians since Gnosticism is creeping back into the church. We need to learn from Scripture and early church fathers as they have already dealt with these problems. Knowing how they fought against the Gnostic heresies will help us do the same today.

Chapter Six

Biblical Forgiveness

What you are about to read is a small portion of my testimony. It is a very helpful snippet from my life to lead into this next topic. If you haven't read my testimony on my website yet, this might come as a bit of a shock to you.

Before we got married, I lied to my wife about something that I was immensely ashamed about. You see, I had purchased the services of prostitutes prior to dating Jenn, who would later become my wife. Before we ever started dating, I suggested we share testimonies. We did, and I said that I had purchased the services of *a* prostitute while I was deployed in Bahrain when the truth was much different. I had actually been with several prostitutes, all while in the United States. I was especially ashamed that I wasn't even away from my homeland when I did this. At least I would have had the excuse that I was lonely if I had done it in Bahrain. Ultimately, it weighed heavily on me that I had lied but not enough for me to confess until nearly a year later.

When I finally did confess, I warned her that what I was about to say would hurt. When I finished telling her what I had done, she told me that it did indeed hurt immensely, but then she got quiet for a moment. After a bit, she said something very simple. She said, "I forgive you." Just those three words. You couldn't imagine the weight that lifted off my shoulders when she said that. How could she forgive me like that? How can we forgive others like that? This chapter will demonstrate that, contrary to popular belief and most Christian scholarship, biblical forgiveness *requires* repentance, and that is precisely how she was able to forgive me like that.

To begin with, let's look at the largest set of teachings on forgiveness. I am putting the entire passage in the book simply because it makes sure that we are all on the same page, and you don't have to go find your Bible now. Matthew 18:10–35 says,

> See that you do not despise one of these little ones. For I tell you that in heaven their angels always see the face of my Father who is in heaven. What do you think? If a man has a hundred sheep, and one of them has gone astray, does he not leave the ninety-nine on the mountains and go in search of the one that went astray? And if he finds it, truly, I say to you, he rejoices over it more than over the ninety-nine that never went astray. So it is not the will of my Father who is in heaven that one of these little ones should perish. If your brother sins against you, go and tell him his fault, between you and him alone. If he listens to you, you have gained your brother. But if he does not listen, take one or two others along with you, that every charge may be established by the evidence of two or three witnesses. If he refuses to listen to them, tell it to the church. And if he refuses to listen even to the church, let him be to you as a Gentile and a tax collector. Truly, I say to you, whatever you bind on earth shall be bound in heaven, and whatever you loose on earth shall be loosed in heaven. Again I say to you, if two of you agree on earth about anything

they ask, it will be done for them by my Father in heaven. For where two or three are gathered in my name, there am I among them. Then Peter came up and said to him, "Lord, how often will my brother sin against me, and I forgive him?" Jesus said to him, "I do not say seven times, but seventy-seven times. Therefore the kingdom of heaven may be compared to a king who wished to settle accounts with his servants. When he began to settle, one was brought to him who owed him ten thousand talents. And since he could not pay, his master ordered him to be sold, with his wife and children and all that he had, and payment to be made. So the servant fell on his knees, imploring him, "Have patience with me, and I will pay you everything." And out of pity for him, the master of that servant released him and forgave him the debt. But when that same servant went out, he found one of his fellow servants who owed him a hundred denarii, and seizing him, he began to choke him, saying, "Pay what you owe." So his fellow servant fell down and pleaded with him, "Have patience with me, and I will pay you." He refused and went and put him in prison until he should pay the debt. When his fellow servants saw what had taken place, they were greatly distressed, and they went and reported to their master all that had taken place. Then his master summoned him and said to him, "You wicked servant! I forgave you all that debt because you pleaded with me. And should not you have had mercy on your fellow servant, as I had mercy on you?" And in anger his master delivered him to the jailers, until he should pay all

his debt. So also my heavenly Father will do to every one of
you, if you do not forgive your brother from your heart.

Before we look at this idea of forgiveness, let me first ask you: Did you see forgiveness without repentance anywhere in this passage? I sure didn't. What we do see is the pursuit of the one who has lost their way. We also see sin within the church, and how to deal with it, which boils down to this: If a brother wrongs you, confront him; if he repents, then you have won back your brother. If he does not listen, take two or three others along; and if he does not listen even to them, confront him before the church. If he *still* doesn't listen, then treat him as you would a tax collector or a pagan. The last part simply means that the unrepentant brother must be treated as an unbeliever because he has demonstrated that he is unwilling to listen to God and the church.[1] If he is in a leadership position and has refused to listen to the church, he must be removed from that position, for he has demonstrated that he doesn't keep to what he professes to believe. In extreme cases, he is to be excommunicated.[2] The final parable tells us how God has forgiven believers, and how we, in turn, are called to forgive others.

At this point, we need to define forgiveness. Different ideas can be labeled as forgiveness. For example, in psychology and sociology, forgiveness is generally something that is done only within your own heart. This is a popular belief among Christians as well, and a common teaching

---

1. Whether this involves an actual loss of salvation is not the subject of this chapter and as such I will not address it. The important thing to remember for our purposes here is that the goal is to bring the offending brother back into reconciliation with those who have been wronged.

2. See the next chapter for more on this.

among Christian counselors. For example, in *The Quick Reference Guide to Biblical Counseling*, Tim Clinton and Ron Hawkins give an outline for forgiving someone that, at most, involves "publicly" forgiving someone by telling friends and/or family, or writing a letter to the offender that does not get sent.[3] By this method, we need not involve the offender at all. This is the idea that if you have forgiven the other person in your heart, then they are forgiven. This is a variation of the view that God (and thus man) forgives unconditionally.[4] Unfortunately, this concept of forgiveness is, simply, not biblical forgiveness. It is only one-half of biblical forgiveness. It is more of a selfish act at this point if you stop here. We have forgiveness offered but no actual forgiveness. In order for forgiveness to *be* forgiveness, it has to be received as well. Biblical forgiveness, as will be seen below, is some form of *conditional* forgiveness.[5] Let's go through a quick list of what biblical forgiveness *is not*:

1. It is not forbearance, long-suffering, or patience. While each of these are things we are called to practice, and they are related to forgiveness to an extent, they are different disciplines. These disciplines mean that we are willing to overlook small wrongs and to be patient with our fellow humans who are not perfect. For example, rather than kill us where we stand when we sin, God is patient in order that we might come to him in repentance.

2. It is not forgetting. We have all heard the phrase "forgive and

---

3. Tim Clinton and Ron Hawkins, *The Quick Reference Guide to Biblical Counseling: Personal and Emotional Issues* (Grand Rapids, MI: Baker Books, 2009), 127.

4. Erikson, *Christian Theology*, 909.

5. Ibid.

forget," right? Well, let me tell you something. That phrase is impossible, at least in the sense that we can somehow banish the wrong from our minds entirely. Not even God forgets our sins in this way. He casts them as far as the east is from the west, but that isn't very far to an omnipresent and omniscient God. Look at it this way: if God is all-knowing, then he literally can't forget something. If he *can* forget something, then he is no longer all-knowing. Why would we, as humans be commanded to do something that even God does not do? What God *does* do is he simply does not bring our sin to mind (which is what the Hebrew word for "remember" means). He *knows* we sinned but doesn't hold it against us. Likewise, we will always *know* someone sinned against us, but if we have forgiven them we no longer deliberately bring it to mind.

3. It is not a selfish act. What this means is that we should forgive others because we love them and God *not* because we seek relief from stress, anger, or pain. Forgiveness is, at its core, an act of love. When Jesus died on the cross to make it possible for us to be forgiven for all our sins, he did it out of love. The Father sent his Son to die so that we could be forgiven and reconciled to him because he loves us beyond what we could possibly imagine (John 3:16). So, if we are forgiving someone to free ourselves of pain, anger, hate, or self-loathing, we are doing something counter to what God does. Forgiveness needs to be done out of love for the other person and love for God. One of the benefits of forgiveness is that we can be free from those feelings, but those feelings *cannot* be the focus of forgiveness.

4. It is not the private, solitary act of an individual heart. There must be at least two people involved: the forgiver and the forgiven.

Now let's look at a quick list of things that biblical forgiveness *is*:

1. It is a commitment to pardon the offender. Whatever was done against you can no longer be held against someone that you have forgiven. For example, if my wife cheats on me and I forgive her, I cannot hold it against her any longer. This is why the next point is so important.

2. It more resembles a spoken contract between the offender and the offended. By that, I mean that both people are bringing something to the table. The offender is bringing repentance, and the offended is bringing the willingness and ability to forgive.

3. It is reconciliation. If there is no reconciliation between the offender and the offended, then the forgiveness given is false. To put this another way, reconciliation is the fruit of forgiveness. It is the purpose of forgiveness. The *reason* we are forgiven by God and called to forgive others is so that we can be reconciled to God and others. The second God forgives us sinners when we repent and turn to him, we are immediately reconciled to him. This is despite the fact that we have proven over and over again that we are sinful and are likely to sin again. Likewise, human forgiveness involves immediate reconciliation.

4. It is an immediate restoration of trust. Yes, I said exactly what I meant to say. This goes along with the last point. Regardless of what we all believe on the particulars of forgiveness, we all agree

that forgiveness is no longer holding someone's sin against them. Is it possible to release someone from what they have done against you and then not reinstate the former level of trust that you had in them because of what they have done against you? *No*, that is an oxymoron. How can I forgive someone and at the same time not trust them because of what I have forgiven them for? I cannot. If I do not trust them, then I, quite simply, didn't forgive them. I am still holding their sin against them. This is *why* repentance must happen because we cannot stop holding someone's sin against them, thus trusting them again, if they haven't repented! We must trust that they are truly repentant before we can forgive them. The second God forgives you, he *expects* you to sin no longer. We still sin, but he trusts us because we have become a new creation that *desires* to do his will. Thus, when we sin against him, he will rebuke us so that we can come back into a relationship with him by admitting that we were wrong and will not do it again. We are to do the same for those who sin against us.

Let's look at the idea of forgiveness offered. Forgiveness offered means that the offended person is *willing* and *ready* to forgive the offender. It means they *desire* to forgive and have been seeking out the one who offended them to be reconciled to them, but until the forgiveness has been asked for and received by the offender, they have not been forgiven. The only way that an offender can receive forgiveness is if they are repentant and ask the one they offended for forgiveness. This brings to mind the parable of the unmerciful servant.

Before we go any further, we need to look at something very important. We are called to forgive as God forgave us. What does that mean? Well, with the exception of Jesus on the cross when he said, "Father, forgive them, for they know not what they do," we have no indication that God ever forgives without repentance. Even this passage doesn't necessarily teach forgiveness without repentance. After all, Jesus only asked that their sin of killing him be forgiven. There is no indication that they *were* forgiven by the Father. The key to this verse is that "they know not what they do." Jesus is saying that the prophecies of his death must be fulfilled. Thus, they know not what they do. It is a very specific situation and, like I said above, there isn't actually any evidence that the Father forgave them for that sin. Now if they repented of that sin, God would immediately forgive them. Some people mention Stephen as another example of forgiveness without repentance (Acts 7:54–60), but that passage only shows that Stephen was willing to forgive them. Again, we have no evidence of actual forgiveness.

What we do know is that God doesn't forgive us our sins if we aren't repentant. Acts 3:19 says, "Repent and be baptized every one of you in the name of Jesus Christ for the forgiveness of your sins," and 1 John 1:9 says, "If we confess our sins [repent], he is faithful and just to forgive us our sins to cleanse us from all unrighteousness." He has done everything short of forcing us to repent. He sent his only Son as a perfect sacrifice so there was nothing that could stop us from being reconciled to him. God has never stopped seeking to be reconciled to us. He is *always* in a posture to forgive, eagerly awaiting the chance to forgive sinners.

So, if God requires repentance prior to forgiveness, why does the church teach that those who are created in his image must forgive even when the offender is unrepentant? Some even go so far as *acknowledging* that God forgives *differently* than humans are supposed to. Tim Clinton and Ron Hawkins write, "[Forgiveness] does not wait for the offender to repent. *Unlike God*, who provides forgiveness when we repent, humans cannot demand repentance before granting forgiveness."[6] They fully acknowledge that God *requires* repentance in order for forgiveness to happen and yet somehow want to argue that humans are not to follow him in this area. Scripture firmly argues against them. Luke 17:3–4 is the parallel passage to the one we have been looking at, but it is much more concise and uses very straightforward language. In it, Jesus says,

> Pay attention to yourselves! If you brother sins, rebuke him, and if he repents, forgive him, and if he sins against you seven times in the day, and turns to you seven times, saying, "I repent," you must forgive him.

"And if he repents"—it doesn't get any clearer than that. However, it also points out that you and I are to forgive those who *repeatedly* sin against us and repent *even within the same day*. This is true regardless of how many times said brother repents. Of course, there is an argument to be made about this. If it becomes obvious that the one who is sinning is intentionally sinning and "repenting" to get out of the consequences, we are to call that out. That is an abuse of the model of biblical forgiveness. This can be challenging to rightly spot. However, we can safely assume that this is the case if someone continues to do the same thing that they said they were sorry for and wouldn't do again. Repentance, by nature, involves changing our behavior. If "repentance" does not result in a change within someone, then it was not true repentance, but merely a confession. That said, we need to be careful here. As we know, humans are not perfect. Even

---

6. Clinton and Hawkins, *The Quick Reference Guide to Biblical Counseling*, 124. Emphasis added.

the most sincere repentance can still result in repeated sin. If someone sins against me and repents and I forgive them and they do the same thing a few years later, that is different from them doing the same thing a day or a few hours later. Occasionally though, sin can be so ingrained in someone that they could truly be trying to change but it will just take a ton of work. For example, a compulsive liar is going to really struggle to break that habit. We need to make sure that we are giving people grace in this.

So, what does all of this mean for us? We must offer forgiveness (that is, we must have a willingness and desire to be reconciled to those who wrong us). We must always seek ways to be reconciled to those who wrong us. If and when they repent, we must be quick to show mercy by forgiving them and holding their sin against them no more. At that point, forgiveness has truly happened.

Possible Exceptions

What if you aren't able to talk to the one who sinned against you, or that person remains unrepentant until the day they die, or they don't believe that they have done wrong? Let me give you a quick scenario. Suppose a woman was raped in an alley by a guy. He didn't know who she was, and she didn't know who he was. How can she be set free from the anger, hate, and self-loathing that she feels if they never meet again? Well, first off, she needs to *want to forgive* him. At this point, she must understand the biblical principle that God is an avenger. She must understand that if the rapist is never repentant, God will deal with the sin. Romans 12:19 says, "Beloved, never avenge yourselves, but leave it to the wrath of God, for it is written, 'Vengeance is mine, I will repay, says the Lord.'" The sin will *not* go unpunished. God will deal with the man if he is never repentant. If you don't believe me, here are some additional verses to look up: Deuteronomy 32:35, Proverbs 20:22, 24:29, Psalm 94:1–2, 1 Peter 2:21–23, and Hebrews 10:30. None of those verses speak about forgiveness; only that God will avenge us. Therefore, the woman can now rest in the fact that God will deal with him if she is unable to forgive him. The debt is still owed, but she has trusted God to deal with the sin appropriately so that if the rapist repents but is unable to find the woman he raped, *he* can still be forgiven. If he doesn't repent, God will deal with the sin.

Conclusion and Warning

After all of this, you might ask: Why does God hate it when we, as Christians, don't forgive others who are repentant? Well, if we look back at the parable of the unmerciful servant, we see that God paid an extremely high price to forgive us of our sins against him. He sent his Son to die for our sins. We cannot take that lightly. We all owed God an insurmountable debt, but because of his desire to be back in a relationship with us, he made a way for us to be forgiven. He *willingly* sacrificed his Son to restore our relationship with him. Thus, when we take his gift and do not share even the smallest portion of that gift with others in our lives who sin against us, he gets very angry, and rightly so. Nothing that can happen to us can compare with what we have done to him.

I must give a warning now. It is impossible to forgive someone who is unrepentant. However, we should always be willing to forgive them and do everything we can to bring them to repentance. That said, if and when they come up to you and repent for a wrong they committed against you and you do not forgive them, you are the unmerciful servant from the last parable in Matthew 18. Jesus makes it clear that you are *worse* than the one who has wronged you because God has forgiven you of an insurmountable debt, and yet you failed to forgive someone who has only slightly wronged you in comparison. The only way to avoid this is to be humble and ask God to help you have a heart that desires to be reconciled to others.

So my challenge to you is that you always be willing and ready to forgive those who sin against you and to give them that forgiveness if they ask for it so that when someone surprises you (like I surprised my wife) and actually seeks you out for forgiveness, you can give them that forgiveness. Additionally, "do not let the sun go down on your anger" (Ephesians 4:26). We need to be willing to confront the people who have sinned against us, especially our brothers and sisters in Christ. On the flip side, if you wronged someone, "If you are offering your gift at the altar and there remember that your brother has something against you, leave your gift there before the altar and go. First be reconciled to your brother, and then come and offer your gift" (Matthew 5:23–24). We need to be zealous about repenting for our sins. Go to the one you have wronged as soon as you think of it and beg their forgiveness.

Chapter Seven

Biblical Church Discipline

A Necessary Part of a Healthy Church

Many churches today either do not understand church discipline or fail to implement it in a significantly impactful way. Theologian Jeremy M. Kimble writes, "Due to misapplications and misunderstandings, discipline has been largely ignored by many congregations, resulting in communities of faith that neglect many of the moral absolutes laid out in Scripture."[1] This is highly detrimental to the church and most often results in weak and/or sinful congregations that are not effective in pursuing Christ and the gospel. But how do we combat this? This chapter will give a biblical understanding of what church discipline is and demonstrates that biblical church discipline is a necessary part of church life that cannot be downplayed if one desires a healthy church.

The Problem

Many churches struggle with church discipline either from a doctrinal standpoint or in practically applying it. Below are two major challenges to

---

1. Jeremy M. Kimble, *40 Questions About Church Membership and Discipline* (Grand Rapids, MI: Kregel Academic, 2017), 33.

effective discipline that churches face today. These are not exhaustive by any means, but they do a good job of demonstrating the issue at hand.

False Understanding of Judging

In contemporary Christianity, judging someone is almost always seen as something sinful. Of course, this causes *significant* problems when it comes to implementing, or even teaching about church discipline. After all, church discipline fundamentally involves judging others' walk with Christ. Since Christians in Western countries commonly believe judging is a sin, we are fighting an uphill battle in trying to bring effective church discipline back into the church. However, church discipline is biblical. Paul writes, "For what have I to do with judging outsiders? Is it not those inside the church whom you are to judge? God judges those outside. 'Purge the evil person from among you'" (1 Corinthians 5:12–13). In his commentary on this epistle, Leon Morris notes, "It was their [the Corinthians] responsibility to discipline their own members."[2] Ultimately, judging goes hand-in-hand with church discipline.[3]

Too Many Church Options with
Too Little Communication Between Them

Another distinct and quite challenging problem is that there are *so many* churches to choose from and these churches *do not* regularly communicate with each other. Even churches in the same denomination likely have little to no regular communication. This is problematic simply be-

---

2. Leon Morris, *1 Corinthians: An Introduction and Commentary* (Downers Grove, IL: InterVarsity Press, 1985), 94.

3. For a brief biblical defense of judging others see L. J. Anderson, "Why Am I so Judgy?" *L. J. Anderson – Author and Blogger*, February 10, 2023. https://ljandersonbooks.com/2023/02/10/why-am-i-so-judgy/.

cause if a church disciplines someone they can just leave and join another church. I witnessed this happen at a previous church. Someone at another church was disciplined for living a gay lifestyle while being part of the youth group leadership. He was kicked out of that church and came to my church, admitted to some of what happened, and claimed that he had stopped doing what he was doing. The pastor at the time took him at his word and he was allowed to be a youth and children's leader at the church. However, evidence surfaced that he had not, in fact, changed his ways. He simply got better at hiding it. This is about as good of a result as one could expect of church discipline today. At least the new church *knew* about some of the problem. This is not the case in most instances. Generally, a person who is disciplined in one church can just join another with no one the wiser. This significantly undermines the effectiveness of church discipline.

What Is the Biblical View of Church Discipline?

The whole concept of the church is given to us through the words of Scripture which the apostles and other early Christians wrote down. If this is true, we need to understand what the *biblical* view of church discipline is. What did God teach, through his Word, regarding discipline?

Analysis of Matthew 18

Matthew 18 is one of the largest passages on church discipline. Overall, the passage discusses forgiveness between individuals; however, Matthew 18:15–20 specifically relates this to a larger body of people than just the wronged and the one who wronged them.

Begins and (Hopefully) Ends with Individuals

Individual sins, whether done against another or not, should, ideally, stop with no more than two people being involved. This is what is laid out in Matthew 18:15. It always starts with an individual member of the church approaching the one who has sinned in the hopes of bringing the latter to repentance. In a truly healthy church, this is likely to be all it takes to bring someone back around. Of course, this is not always the case which leads to the next section.

Tiered Church Involvement

Matthew 18:15–20 contains one of only a few references to the ἐκκλησία (assembly/church) in the Gospels. This ἐκκλησία is to be involved in the case of individual sin in greater and greater measures until the whole assembly is included if need be. Ultimately, this passage seeks to resolve sin/conflict within a church body by the least possible amount of church involvement. We are *not* to jump immediately to telling the whole church that someone has sinned and needs to be confronted. This would be an abuse of church discipline and is no better than gossiping, which is sinful (Romans 1:29). *Instead*, you and I are to "go and tell him his fault, between you and him alone" (Matthew 18:15). If said brother listens, it stops there as you have "gained your brother." However, if he does not listen, then the next tier of church involvement begins which is to bring one or two others along. If, and only if, this does not work does one involve the whole church.

Sins Not Necessarily Against an Individual in the Church

Though this has been touched on briefly, some sins are not necessarily against an individual. Some are sins that involve a group of people, as is often the case with church leaders who sin. Sometimes, the sin is just against God. Additionally, though it cannot be addressed in this book due to length constraints, modern technology has made it possible for one person to effectively teach potentially *millions* of others. Contemporary church discipline needs to take this into account. How do we deal with someone in the church at large who is sinning or teaching falsely to those within our own congregation when they are technically not part of said congregation?

Does Matthew 18 Still Apply Here?

Matthew 18 does, for the most part, apply perfectly well in the above-mentioned situations. The only area that it may not apply to would be dealing with false teaching on the internet especially considering that it does not specifically say that the sin was done to an individual. Though some texts have the addition of "against you" in Matthew 18:15, many critical texts *do not* contain this phrase and thus it is likely to be an addition.[4] Therefore, it is perfectly reasonable to view Matthew 18:15 as saying that if a brother sees another brother sin, he ought to confront him about it even if that sin is not directly against him.

What Does the Punishment Look Like?

Rebuking/Confronting the Offender

At the very least, the punishment for church discipline involves confrontation and/or rebuke. This is to be done in love with the motive of winning back one's brother. Christians, when they see sin amongst fellow believers, are not to turn a blind eye. Turning a blind eye is actually *not* a loving thing to do as it allows said believer to live in sin and backslide away from God and the body of Christ and potentially end up turning away from God. Loving Christians confront their brothers and sisters just as the writer of Hebrews said of man and God, "It is for discipline that

---

4. France, *Matthew: An Introduction and Commentary*, 277.

you have to endure. God is treating you as sons. For what son is there whom his father does not discipline? If you are left without discipline, in which all have participated, then you are illegitimate children and not sons" (Hebrews 12:7–8) and later, "For the moment all discipline seems painful rather than pleasant, but later it yields the peaceful fruit of righteousness to those who have been trained by it" (Hebrews 12:11). Because God confronts and disciplines Christians, so too are Christians to confront and discipline one another.

Excommunication

"How can a person leave a church? The short answer is by death, by joining another gospel-preaching church, or by church discipline."[5] This quote is from a chapter on church membership, but it elucidates an important point on church discipline. Christians are to be part of a church <u>*always*</u>. The only way to leave a church, outside of death or moving to another church, is by being disciplined. I would hazard a guess that most Protestant Christians would immediately think of the Roman Catholic church upon hearing *excommunication*. It is not a word that gets passed about much in Protestant circles. That being said, there is absolutely a biblical precedence for this consequence of unrepentant sin in the church. In fact, this seems to have been expected a fair amount in the early church based on the references in Scripture. It happens when someone is treated as an unbeliever and/or is actively avoided by the church. In contemporary Western churches, this would involve being removed from formal church membership and no longer being allowed to participate in various ministry activities or church governance. It seems rare that it goes to the point of

---

5. Daniel L. Akin, David S. Dockery, and Nathan A. Finn, eds., *A Handbook of Theology* (Brentwood, TN: B&H Academic, 2023), 445.

true expulsion from the church building though this is closer to the idea as it is found in Scripture.[6] Interestingly though, there was a church split that happened over this exact issue.[7] Should a church kick out those who have been disciplined or merely remove them from positions of leadership? Also, what is the main characteristic of sin that allows for excommunication? In his book on church discipline, Jonathan Leeman writes, "Only those sins which are *outward, significant, and unrepentant* warrant public exposure and excommunication."[8] While he argues that all three *must* be present for excommunication to be warranted, this goes against Matthew 18:15–20, which suggests that only *unrepentant* sin is needed. A believer who is made aware of his sin and yet refuses to repent of it even when confronted by the entire church is to be excommunicated. This is simply because said person is actively and willingly disobeying God.

The Focus Is Always *on Reconciliation*

The punishments given in each and every case in Scripture have the end goal of repentance and reconciliation. In their book on church leadership, John Hammett and Benjamin Merkle state, "The hope of the church is that discipline will lead to repentance and restoration."[9] Even excommu-

---

6. For example, 2 John 1:10–11 states that one is to not even greet a person who brings a different teaching for that would be partaking in their evil works.

7. See, Kirk R. McGregor, "Biblical Inerrancy, Church Discipline, and the Mennonite-Amish Split," *Journal of the Evangelical Theological Society* 60, no. 3 (September 2017): 582, https://go.openathens.net/redirector/liberty.edu?url=https://www.proquest.com/scholarly-journals/biblical-inerrancy-church-discipline-mennonite/docview/1964554361/se-2.

8. Jonathan Leeman, *Understanding Church Discipline* (Nashville, TN: B&H Books, 2016), 43.

9. John S. Hammatt and Benjamin L. Merkle, eds, *Those Who Must Give an Account: A Study of Church Membership and Church Discipline* (Nashville, TN: B&H Academic, 2012), 19.

nication and treating someone as an unbeliever are still focused on the hope that doing so will drive the condemned person *back* into fellowship with God and the church. Though this is the hope, practically speaking, this does not always happen. Christians need to be aware of the possibility that church discipline might fail to produce reconciliation as it can be extremely discouraging.

Why Is Church Discipline Necessary?

So, church discipline is biblical, but many would still say that it is overly judgmental to put it into practice. While church discipline *can* be done improperly, it is still necessary regardless. Jonathan Leeman writes, "Broadly speaking, discipline is necessary whenever a disciple departs from the way of Christ by sinning."[10] This is absolutely true; however, it is important to break that down somewhat while also realizing that this does not cover all of church discipline.

Protecting the Church from Heresy

The first major reason for church discipline is that it protects the church from heresy. Mostly this is because it involves someone who is *teaching* a false doctrine rather than merely believing or practicing it. Scripture warns that false teachers and prophets will come into the church secretly bringing with them destructive heresies (Matthew 7:15 and 2 Peter 2:1, for example). These people will look like believers but are instead "ravenous wolves" (Matthew 7:15). Church discipline *should* be used to protect the flock from such people. They may not submit themselves to the

---

10. Jonathan Leeman, *Church Discipline: How the Church Protects the Name of Jesus* (Wheaton, IL: Crossway, 2012), 48.

leaders of a local church for discipline, but the congregation ought to trust the word of the leaders enough to avoid such people. This is also heavily related to church unity. The spread of heresy within a church is a direct attack on the unity of said church. This church will have to focus serious attention inwardly to deal with the problem which in turn takes away from the church's mission in the Great Commission (Matthew 28:19–20). That is not to say that heresy should be *ignored* to fulfill the Great Commission. Rather, it means that when heresy raises its ugly head it is necessary to meet it quickly head-on in order to get back to the mission.

Preventing Individual Apostasy

This reason is more in line with what Leeman was talking about in his quote. Church discipline helps prevent apostasy in individual believers. When one believer sins, the church should correct him to get him back on the right path. Failure to do so can result in a complete falling away from Christ. Christians are, in a sense, our brother's keeper (Genesis 4:9). It is the church community that gives the most help in preventing or fixing individual apostasy, outside of God himself. Even considering God, this does not change much since God typically uses fellow Christians. Consider, for example, Paul's rebuking of Peter in Galatians 2:11–14. Peter withdrew from hanging around the Gentile believers for fear of the Jewish believers. This was a problem with an individual; however, this particular individual could have caused some significant problems with the unity of the early church had his sin continued.

Practical Ways to Apply Proper Church Discipline

Since church discipline is both as necessary and as neglected as has been argued thus far, we'll discuss two potential ways to move in the right direction.

Two Practical Ways

The first practical way of seeking to address this divide between recognizing the importance of church discipline and putting it into practice is to develop a biblical understanding about church discipline within the congregation. On the surface, this may not seem all that practical, but this is truly the starting point. Jay Adams discusses this as being both positive and negative. He says, "Too often discipline is thought of only in the remedial sense; its promotional and preventative aspects are unrecognized and ignored."[11] Basically, developing a healthy culture of church discipline involves both aspects. Any given church needs to be *very* intentional about teaching biblical church discipline and effectively implementing it. It was noted earlier that most Western Christians have a false understanding of what it means to judge others. Yet, Scripture is quite clear that Christians are to judge those inside the church. This is where church discipline starts. It begins by recognizing the need and expectation of righteously judging one another. Therefore, a church needs to make sure that its leaders and congregants understand the biblical example and mandate properly. If a church has a formal church membership, a solid class on biblical church discipline ought to be a required part of the membership process. If there is no formal membership, there should be regularly offered classes or small

---

11. Jay E. Adams, *Handbook of Church Discipline: A Right and Privilege of Every Church Member* (Grand Rapids, MI: Zondervan, 1986), 22.

groups based around church discipline that are highly encouraged by the church leadership. Additionally, it would behoove churches to spell all of this out, at least briefly, in a statement of faith or church membership documents.[12] Congregants should be able to quickly and easily find this information if needed.

The next practical way to begin implementing effective church discipline involves two areas. First, even if a church has no formal church membership, a church can have a document that gets signed by anyone who wishes to be an active part of the church that details what one should expect regarding church discipline both personally and corporately. The second addresses the previously stated issue of too little communication between churches. That is, if a church does discipline a member and they end up leaving the church or are excommunicated, there's rarely a system in place to keep that individual from joining another church or even ending up in a leadership position there. This means that even when church discipline is effectively implemented in one church, it may fail to protect surrounding churches. Thus, there should be an expectation among churches that when someone wants to be a member or active participant in a church, they need to provide the contact information of someone (preferably a leader of some sort) at their previous church for a reference. In the case of someone who left a church under good terms, it would be worthwhile for everyone to have that church give them a letter that essentially says that they left under good terms. This smooths out the process and even has biblical examples to back it up.[13]

---

12. This could be as simple as a statement that the church teaches and practices church discipline as it is shown in Scripture.

13. See, for example, 3 John 1:12.

Deal with Problems Early!

One of the biggest failures to implement church discipline can be seen in the Roman Catholic Church. Unfortunately, the Catholic Church had thousands of years to build systemic problems within itself. By the time of the Reformation, the Catholic Church was beyond reasonable church discipline. It had a *long* time to solidify its problematic teachings. Had the problems that led to the Reformation been caught in their infancy, it is possible that the Reformation never would have been necessary. The important lesson to be learned is this: Do not let problems fester! Unfortunately, that is exactly what is happening with many churches today as they fail to properly apply church discipline. Instead of working to heal the sick body part, churches too often *ignore* the gangrene that is developing. Gangrene, if left untreated, can lead to loss of limb or the death of the whole person. Likewise, the longer we wait to implement church discipline, the more damaging and catastrophic the results will be once it *is* implemented. Biblically speaking, this is when it becomes necessary to excommunicate individuals or groups. In some cases, if it goes too far, the church as a whole will die. When we see a problem developing, we need to deal with it then and there. Elsewise, the church is liable to split or die. Effective, *early* church discipline can and should be able to prevent most church splits. Unfortunately, this is going to be challenging because church discipline is not and has not been effectively implemented in many churches. Thus, theologian Gregg Allison writes,

> The effort required [to reverse the trend of sliding into moral dissolution and relativism] will be so monumental and controversial that it will cost churches much time to teach on and reinstitute the practice of church discipline, great effort to

apply the recovered practice in the lives of persistently sinning church members, deep repentance on the part of those members and compassionate mercy from churches toward those members, and strong leadership to withstand congregational criticism for the restoration of the practice.[14]

Most churches in the West are already in a state of having let the gangrene spread, often for many years. Thus, even implementing the *idea* of church discipline, much less church discipline itself, will be a distinct challenge for many churches.

Conclusion

Though often misunderstood and thus neglected, church discipline is a necessary part of the life of a healthy church. It is fully biblical and needs to be urgently taught in churches before it gets too difficult to do so. Effective church discipline begins by educating church members on both the preventative and remedial aspects of chuch discipline. Ultimately, church discipline is the only way to maintain a church healthy enough to fulfill the Great Commission.

---

14. Gregg R. Allison, *Sojourners and Strangers: The Doctrine of the Church* (Wheaton, IL: Crossway, 2012), 179-80.

Chapter Eight

Is Christianity a Religion or a Relationship?

I AM PROBABLY GOING to step on many toes with this chapter and, well, that's ok. Sometimes we need our toes to be stepped on to realize that what we are doing and/or teaching is wrong or unhelpful. In recent years, there has been a lot of focus on Christianity being a *relationship* rather than a *religion*. I have seen this idea time and time again. In fact, I have *said* this myself. Granted, I wasn't following God at the time. I was just spouting out what I had heard to look like a Christian. I would say it and have no idea what it meant or whether it was true. That said, this idea has made me uneasy since I started following God. This is because I believe that the emphasis on Christianity being a relationship is extreme. To start this teaching, I am just going to answer the title question straight up. Christianity is both a religion *and* a relationship.

What Makes Christianity a Religion?

I suppose the place to start on this question is to define "religion." There are three main definitions of religion. Depending on the dictionary you use, there will be slight differences. I think all three definitions are accurate for our purposes, so I will address each one. All three definitions below come from the online Merriam-Webster Dictionary.[1]

The first definition is, "the service and worship of God or the supernatural." This is a very broad definition; however, it is *exactly* what Christianity is (though we could do without the "or the supernatural" part). We believe in, are in service to, and worship God.

The second definition is, "a personal set or institutionalized system of religious attitudes, beliefs, and practices." This describes Christianity to a T. Christianity is full of rules whether we like it or not. Scripture commands us to behave in certain ways. There is no way around this.

The final definition is, "a cause, principle, or system of beliefs held to with ardor and faith." Yet again, Christianity fits solidly within this definition. In fact, specific *aspects* of Christianity fit well within this definition. For example, evangelism is a cause that we ought to hold to with ardor and faith. Thus, *evangelism* could rightly be called a "religion" with this definition.

Christianity clearly fits within all three definitions of "religion." Thus, we would be wise to call it as such. It is foolish to refuse to call it what it is simply because we dislike a term. I could understand if Christianity only loosely fits the definition, but that just isn't the case. It is impossible to remove religion from Christianity without seriously compromising it. In recent years, we have seen a reductionist view of Christianity. There is a tendency to reduce it to *just* a relationship or *just* Jesus. This, simply, does not do our faith and our God justice.

---

1. Merriam-Webster.com Dictionary, s.v. "religion," accessed August 18, 2024, https://www.merriam-webster.com/dictionary/religion.

Religion *Is Not* Legalism or Tradition

One issue in the modern church regarding this topic is conflating "religion" with "legalism." While religion *can* turn into legalism, obedience to God is not legalism in and of itself. I have often found it helpful when discussing this topic with someone to try to figure out what they mean by "religion." Often, I find that they use the term in the same place I would use terms such as legalism and traditions. For example, they might be thinking of someone's insistence that hymns are the only valid form of music in a church setting. This is not a "religion" issue; rather, it is an example of tradition becoming legalism. Obedience to the rules God laid out is not legalism, nor is all tradition bad. The issue is when we take a tradition that has been very helpful in our own walk with Christ and tell others that said thing is the *only* way to do it. My dad, for example, has an amazing quiet time every morning. He spends this time reading the Word, praying, and meditating on God and his Word. He can rightly say that all Christians should pray and read and meditate on Scripture, but if he were to say that everyone needs to do it exactly like he does, that would be legalism. He would be elevating a personal tradition to the same level as God's Word. Doing the former is an example of *religion* while doing the latter is an example of *legalism*.

What Makes Christianity a Relationship?

Many, if not all, religions outside of Christianity have a different view of how their god(s) interact with humans and each other. This typically involves either fickle gods who must be appeased (like the Greek gods) or a god who is aloof and unknowable, like Allah. The God of Christianity is radically different than either of these ideas.

Salvation in Christianity is built on John 3:16: "For God so loved the world, that he gave his only Son, that whoever believes in him should not perish but have eternal life" and John 17:3: "And this is eternal life, that they know you, the only true God, and Jesus Christ whom you have sent." Both of these verses demonstrate a fundamental difference between Christianity and other religions. No other deity cares for his subjects enough to be willing to die to save those who would believe in him. Our God loved us enough. He desires to have a relationship with us. We see this from the very beginning of time in Genesis to the end of Scripture in Revelation. It would make for a *very long* chapter if I were to show how this plays out throughout Scripture, so I will limit myself to the beginning and end of the Bible.

The first three chapters of Genesis provide several examples of God's desire to have a relationship with us. In chapters one and two God created Adam and Eve in a way that was significantly more involved and personal than we see with the rest of creation. Genesis 1:26–27 says,

> Then God said, "Let us make man in our image, after our likeness. And let them have dominion over the fish of the sea and over the birds of the heavens and over the livestock and over all the earth and over every creeping thing that creeps on the earth." So God created man in his own image, in the image of God he created him; male and female he created them.

God created us in his own image. We alone are created in his likeness. Also, God gives us dominion over his creation on earth. All of it. This is *not* something you would do with just anyone.

From the opposite end of things, there is Revelation. The book of Revelation primarily deals with the great tribulation and what comes after. As the tribulation and Jesus' thousand-year-reign end, God destroys the heavens and the earth and replaces them with a new heaven and a new earth. On this new earth, God makes his dwelling with us. It is the ultimate plan. There will be a new Jerusalem where he will dwell. Revelation 21:22–27 says,

> And I saw no temple in the city, for its temple is the Lord God the Almighty and the Lamb. And the city has no need of sun or moon to shine on it, for the glory of God gives it light, and its lamp is the Lamb. By its light will the nations walk, and the kings of the earth will bring their glory into it, and its gates will never be shut by day—and there will be no night there. They will bring into it the glory and the honor of the nations. But nothing unclean will ever enter it, nor anyone who does what is detestable or false, but only those who are written in the Lamb's book of life.

Those who are in the Lamb's book of life (i.e., Christians) will dwell forever with our God. It is his desire and his plan to be with us. Not only will he dwell with us, but we will "see his face" (Revelation 22:4). It is very clear that the God of the Bible is a God who desires a relationship with his people.

We can even look at the Trinity itself to see the centrality of relationship in Christianity. God is three-in-one, with the Father, Son, and Holy Spirit together in perfect unity as one God. God, in giving us the Holy Spirit and adoption as his children, has invited us to partake in the relationship within the Trinity. This is amazing to consider. The God who created the universe with nothing but his words desires a relationship with us, his creation. Ultimately, this means that Christianity is *also* a relationship in addition to being a religion.

Attack on "Religion."

There are some Christians, including an entire movement of Christianity, who think there is nothing good about "religion." To these Christians, it is borderline heresy to label Christianity as a religion due to the belief that religion is always bad. However, you may be thinking that the term "religion" is used in the Bible as being a good thing. You would be right. The term doesn't appear all that often, but it *does* appear. In particular, the first chapter of James has three references to religion. Two of them are "θρησκεία" which means "religion," and the other is "θρῆσκος" which means "religious." James 1:26–27 (emphasis added) says,

> If anyone thinks he is *religious* and does not bridle his tongue but deceives his heart, this person's *religion* is worthless. *Religion* that is pure and undefiled before God the Father is this: to visit orphans and widows in their affliction, and to keep oneself unstained from the world.

As you might have noticed, there are two references right there that show that religion isn't automatically a bad thing. Depending on how you look at it, all three indicate that there is such a thing as good religion. "This person's religion is worthless" demonstrates that a particular person (he who doesn't bridle his tongue) has religion that is worthless. Yet, that same reference implies that there is religion that is *not* worthless. James then teaches what a pure and undefiled religion is, meaning that there is such a thing as good religion!

So, we have a direct teaching from Scripture that demonstrates that religion can be a good thing if done right. How, then, do these Christians get around this idea and hold to the belief that all religion is bad? Part of it comes with the ability to just ignore the verses above. Realistically, two verses out of the whole of Scripture isn't much. That said, there are many other words that Christians use that have a solid biblical grounding despite the word itself never being used. For example, "trinity" never appears in Scripture, yet we hold to it regardless because the *concept* is in Scripture. Sometimes Scripture *does* use the specific word in some passages and not in others. However, if the *concept* appears in those other passages then we should include said passages in our attempt to understand the topic.[2] This is true of Christianity being a religion as well. Even if we remove the words that mean "religion" in the Bible, or translate them differently, we can still come to the accurate conclusion that Christianity is, fundamentally, a religion. Yet, somehow, we still see a large group of Christians who view "religion" as always bad. This comes primarily from a faulty understanding of what a religion is, and subsequently, a faulty understanding of Christianity itself.

What happens when you have someone who believes that all religion is bad and decides to publish a translation of Scripture? That might seem like an oddly specific question. Unfortunately, we have exactly that. It

---

2. John S. Hammett, *Biblical Foundations for Baptist Churches: A Contemporary Ecclesiology* (Grand Rapids, MI: Kregel Publications, 2005), 31. The example given by Hammett involves the term ἐκκλησία meaning *church/assembly*.

is called *The Passion Translation*. For those of you who don't know, I am very against this translation for a variety of reasons. However, one of those reasons in particular is that Brian Simmons (the author) wrote this translation with a bias toward his own personal theology. He argues that he didn't do that, but there is significant evidence to suggest otherwise. One example is how he handles James 1:26–27. Brian Simmons belongs to a group of people that many refer to as the "New Apostolic Reformation" or "NAR" for short. This is not a name that they claim themselves, so it is something that I try to avoid using about them. That said, it is a group of people who share similar doctrines and beliefs. They include people like Bill Johnson, Brian Simmons, Benny Hinn, C. Peter Wagner (he technically coined the term "NAR"), and Kris Vallotton, and are examples of Christians who tend to be adamant about religion being bad. Simmons' translation is widely accepted and loved by these people. I believe one of the primary reasons is that their faulty theology now has a Bible "translation" that aligns with it. For example, let's compare James 1:26–27 in the ESV v Simmons' (TPT) version. The ESV says (emphasis added),

> If anyone thinks he is **religious** and does not bridle his tongue but deceives his heart, this person's **religion** is worthless. **Religion** that is pure and undefiled before God the Father is this: to visit orphans and widows in their affliction, and to keep oneself unstained from the world.

James 1:26–27 in TPT says (emphasis added),

> If someone believes they have a **relationship with God** but fails to guard his words then his heart is drifting away and

> his **religion** is shallow and empty. **True spirituality** that is pure in the eyes of our Father God is to make a difference in the lives of the orphans, and widows in their troubles, and to refuse to be corrupted by the world's values.

The differences are pretty obvious. Now, Simmons does have in his notes that verse 26 can be translated similarly to the ESV; however, that has only appeared recently. This passage is one of the ones that he has been getting into trouble over, so he has allowed for the original translation in verse 26. That said, he does *not* acknowledge, in any way, that the third use of "religion," which is at the beginning of verse 27, can be translated as "religion." Why is that? *Because all religion is bad!* You see, verse 26 can be explained away as someone who merely *thinks* they are religious. Verse 27 cannot be seen that way. It directly says that there is religion that is pure and undefiled. This is why Simmons *cannot* allow that there is another way of translating it as "religion." In doing so, he has gotten rid of that pesky passage that says that not all religion is bad, at least for those who read his translation.

Why Does This Matter?

One of the more important reasons this matters is that we honestly look silly to claim that Christianity is not a religion. I understand the desire to emphasize the differences between Christianity and other religions, but we need to do so in a way that is accurate and truthful. The world *knows* that Christianity is a religion because it fits all the definitions of "religion." Yet, we, as Christians, seem to be unwilling to admit the truth of that. It isn't a good look for us. It is a reason for nonbelievers to mock us *fairly*, which we should avoid if at all possible. We should not be giving valid reasons for people to mock us and God. Instead, let us hold to the truth in our speech and actions so that when we are mocked or slandered it is done unfairly and will put the slanderer to shame (1 Peter 3:16).

Chapter Nine

Religious Freedom

The Silent Killer

Beware, beware, the lulling croon
The voice that calls beckoning
For asleep, will you be soon
If you should listen unknowing

Let him who has ears hear
Let the one with understanding know
The silent killer of man is here
His song fills the world with woe

A slow poison to the sons of light
And sure death to the sons of the dark
Is the song that brings the fight
To slow the spread of the Light's spark

It stands as one pure and good
And those it kills praise its name

But vastly misunderstood
And underestimated the same

The children of light need not fear death's sting
But the song calls quietly to the children
They listen to its music and begin to sing
Thus, pain and death become the villain

The children have listened too long
They know not the danger they're in
Too often have they sung death's song
They languish in its din

"A servant is not greater than his master"
This, the sons of light know
Yet the croon spells disaster
For persecution, they wish to forgo

Unlike their master, they wish to be
In this one area they do chafe
The song whispers his lies with glee
That from all danger they shall be safe

Yet never were they called to safety
No! To hatred from the world, they were called
The burden given to them is weighty
At their complacency, they should be appalled

But they are not appalled
They fight harder than ever for the lullaby
By which they have been enthralled
The music that causes some to sleep and others to die

Learn well the song's tune
That you might not fall for the charm
Understand the song's quiet croon
Hear it and sound the alarm!

Wake the sleeping ones!
Wake them and strengthen the weak!
A name have I for the sons
Religious Freedom is the one of which I speak

"What cannot be denied is that religious liberty is important and may be the most essential of freedoms."[1] This statement from a contemporary theology book is an interesting one. In agreement with this quote, many would argue that the United States has been blessed with religious freedom since it was founded. I would argue that the opposite is more likely to be

---

1. Akin et al., *A Handbook of Theology*, 559.

true. It is possible that the above quote is referencing religious freedom from the angle of not making Christianity a state-enforced religion. If that is the case, I would agree. However, based on the context of that quotation, I do not believe that's what the authors mean. This chapter addresses that issue but more broadly focuses on religious freedom as it is espoused contemporarily in popular culture. Though the concept seems to be a good thing on the surface, this chapter seeks to demonstrate that religious freedom is not only impossible to implement, but also detrimental to the growth of Christian disciples.

Religious Freedom Is Good in Nearly All Cases

For every religion out there, except maybe Islam and Christianity, religious freedom is undoubtedly a good thing. Whether that's Buddhism, Hinduism, Satanism, Judaism, any of the myriad paganistic religions, or even atheism and agnosticism, most religions are *not* based on trying to get others to follow their religion. For a Hindu to seek converts is a far-fetched idea. They are happy being left alone to worship their own way. But to Islam, conversion is vastly important. This conversion can be effected through either violence or peaceable conversion. For example, Qur'an 9:5–6 states,

> But when the forbidden months are past, then fight and slay the Pagans wherever ye may find them, and seize them, beleaguer them, and lie in wait for them in every stratagem (of war). But if they repent, and establish regular prayers, and pay Zakat then open the way for them: For Allah is Oft-forgiving, Most Merciful. If one amongst the Pagans ask

thee for asylum, grant it to him, so that he may hear the Word of Allah; and then escort him to where he can be secure, that is because they are men without knowledge (Abdullah Yusuf Ali's translation).

As can quickly be seen, these verses demonstrate that Islam is to advance itself both militarily and peaceably. The first verse (verse 5) is arguably one of the most important verses in the Qur'an, especially as it relates to jihad.[2] Generally speaking, following Muhammad's teachings and the Qur'an, non-Muslims are to be either forced or coerced to convert or killed. It is not in the nature of the Islamic believer to allow others to worship what they want without trying to convert them either violently or peacefully. What is interesting is that, in the case of Islam, the USA does *not* allow its followers religious freedom. ISIS teachings closely follow and resemble the true teachings of Mohammad and we bombed the crap out of them. The USA is only tolerant of the Islamic people who *don't* follow Mohammad as commanded, those who treat jihad as only a personal struggle against sin. But that is not the topic of this chapter. This was simply to explain why I included Islam in the group that might not find value in religious freedom. It also demonstrates a problem with religious freedom that I will address later.

So, is religious freedom good for Christianity? I have spent many hours dwelling on this question. On the one hand, I have always been grateful

---

2. David Cook, *Understanding Jihad* (Berkley: University of California Press, 2015), 10. This book engages jihad as a whole and notes that there are various levels of jihad that do not necessarily align with only the "holy war" angle often espoused by non-Muslims or the personal fight against sin angle often espoused by Western Muslims.

that I can worship God without being thrown in prison, beaten, or murdered. But I have also studied Scripture and history, and both point to religious freedom as being bad for the church. Additionally, history shows that it is *very* bad for Christianity to be *the* religion. Before engaging with the former question, let me first talk about how that last sentence works.

Christianity being *the* religion of a country or even the world is very detrimental to the church. Theoretically, the exact opposite is true; however, like communism, it is much better on paper than it is in real life. Wherever Christianity has become the religion of the state, there is massive corruption within the church. Politics enter into the church and the church dies from the inside out. Notice what I am arguing. I am not arguing against Christians being politicians. Being a Christian in politics is a *good* thing. It is very good to have Christian values at the very top of the leadership within a country. Rather, I am arguing that bringing *any* politics into the *church* is playing with fire. The early church was thriving (albeit through persecution) until Emperor Constantine began the transition to making Christianity the dominant religion. Once that started happening, Christianity began to decay. Obviously, there were still strong Christians throughout history, but all kinds of evil came from the church taking a role in leading the world. Most of the problem comes from the fact that we aren't perfect. So, while we might start with the best intentions, we all are unlikely to stay strong against the sway of power. Once the church could be used for means of political gain, it was only a matter of time before it started to be used that way. Also, when Christianity is forced on people, they will most often become false converts, believers in name alone. It is not possible to force someone to believe something that they do not want to believe.

The Value of Religious Freedom

One thing that cannot be denied is that there are some benefits of religious freedom. That is not in question here. The question is whether the positives outweigh the negatives. To answer that, we must first look at the positive side of things.

Adheres to What Is Theoretically True

From a broad perspective, humans have *always* had religious freedom. At every point in history, any given human has been "free" to choose whatever he or she wants regarding religion. Some choices may have resulted in people being killed, beaten, or suffering some other punishment, but the fact remains that everyone has been free to choose their religion. This is similar to the idea that I am "free" to murder someone if I so choose. I have the ability to do so and no one could really stop me if I did make that choice. However, if I were caught, the *consequences* of me murdering someone are severe. Beyond that, I have no desire whatsoever to murder anyone. This does not detract from the fact that I could *freely* make the choice to do so if I wanted. This is simply the concept of freewill. Every human has the freedom to choose what they want to believe and practice. Whether we get into *trouble* for believing or doing that thing does not matter. No one can *force* me to be an atheist. They could try to persuade me, even at gunpoint if they wanted to, but they cannot *force* the belief in Jesus out of me. This is also true of the opposite. I cannot force someone to be a Christian. Attempts have been made in the past to do this very thing, and attempts have been made to stamp out Christianity. Both have been unsuccessful in the majority of cases. And, in essentially all cases, if they did succeed, it was in word only.

Freedom to Worship without Threat

The biggest advantage to religious freedom, at least on the surface, is the ability to worship without threat of murder, rape, beatings, imprisonment, etc. In the United States, I can believe whatever the heck I want and have no reasonable threat to my safety. However, this is not true when it comes to *practicing* religion. I can *believe* whatever I want, but I cannot *practice* whatever I want.

The Problems with Religious Freedom

The concept of religious freedom is valuable in some regards, especially regarding religions that do not need to proselytize. However, the concept does not come without problems and challenges. Below, I will look at a few of the major concerns I have with religious freedom from a Christian perspective.

True Religious Freedom Is Impossible

As mentioned above, Islam, as it is meant to be practiced, is *not* a religion that can be freely practiced according to Western standards. Islamic adherents are *supposed* to forcibly convert non-believers, nearly by any means necessary. This can include what most of the world would consider murder and/or terrorism. The obvious conclusion is that there must be limits on what a religion can practice. A pagan religion that involves human sacrifice, for example, cannot be practiced as it goes against the established law against murder. Likewise, Christianity holds to certain beliefs that are culturally unacceptable or even legally unacceptable in some cases. During the COVID-19 pandemic, gatherings were, in many cases, illegal. Christianity holds God's commands *above* the commands of men and God has *commanded* that Christians meet together regularly (see

Hebrews 10:25 for an example). Thus, Christians could, and should from a biblical perspective, disregard the laws against gathering together. Yet, this was not legal to do. True religious freedom would mean that any religion could freely, without consequences, practice whatever it is that the religion teaches. This has not been, nor ever will be, the case with religious freedom. Not only that, but it has the potential to create complete anarchy. If *anyone* can get away with *anything* in the name of religion, even a made-up one, then chaos ensues. A rapist can simply say that he rapes women in accord with his religion. A thief can steal whatever he wants provided he does so in the name of his god. True religious freedom has never existed and will never exist.

Another important factor here is that the culture today is primarily secular. The culture goes against Scripture in many ways. A couple of major examples can be seen in the abortion and LGBTQ debates. These lines are almost entirely drawn with Christians on one side and non-Christians on the other.[3] This secular culture is anti-Christian in many ways. We are constantly seeing attacks against Christianity's freedom when Christianity teaches something different from what the culture does. We are told to keep our practices to ourselves. Basically, we have the freedom of religion only so long as it doesn't affect anyone else. This leads directly into the next section.

Evangelism Has Been Demonized

Likely a logical outplaying of the concept of religious freedom is that anyone who actively tries to convert someone from one religion to another is treading on the other person's religious freedom. This is not where the idea of religious freedom began. The legal scholar, John Witte, writes, "The

---

3. There are significant exceptions to this; however, it is generally the way things play out.

founders embraced the ancient Western principle of liberty of conscience. For them, liberty of conscience protected religious voluntarism—'the unalienable right of private judgment in matters of religion,' the freedom to choose, change, or discard one's religious beliefs, practices, or associations."[4] He goes on to discuss how someone's religious belief was to be "fashioned" by their "reason, will, and experience."[5] An important thing to note here is that this does *not* preclude proselytizing. It merely precludes someone from being *forced* to adhere to one religion or another or suffer death or some other serious consequence. However, from a contemporary perspective, this is not how it plays out. If I evangelize to someone who does not want to hear what I believe, I could get into trouble for attempting to "force" my religion on someone else. Religious freedom, then, has attacked a Christian's ability to follow God's command to "go therefore and make disciples" (Matthew 28:19). The original concept of religious freedom is different from the contemporary interpretation.

The Expectation of Freedom of Practice without Consequences Is Antibiblical

Scripture warns us on many occasions that we *will* be persecuted and hated by the world. The fact that we simply aren't at this point, at least in the West, is a mark against us. It demonstrates that we are not living according to how we are expected to live. Jesus doesn't tell us that we *may* face persecution for following him. He says we *will* be both persecuted and hated. If Christians in the West were to truly stand firm and live out our faith, I am confident we would see persecution come—potentially very

---

4. John Witte, Jr., *The Blessings of Liberty: Human Rights and Religious Freedom in the Western Legal Tradition* (Cambridge: Cambridge University Press, 2021), 139.

5. Ibid.

heavy persecution. It is firmly anti-biblical to have an expectation of no persecution. Anyone who says otherwise either doesn't know Scripture or is lying through their teeth.

It Easily Produces Lukewarm Christians

The church in the U.S. and many Western countries is very similar to another church that we see in Scripture. The church of Laodicea in Revelation 3 had a problem. They were lukewarm. In Revelation 3:15–17, Jesus says,

> I know your works: you are neither cold nor hot. Would that you were either cold or hot! So, because you are lukewarm, and neither hot nor cold, I will spit you out of my mouth. For you say, I am rich, I have prospered, and I need nothing, not realizing that you are wretched, pitiable, poor, blind, and naked.

The idea of being lukewarm is that of just going through the motions. The church of Laodicea had lost their fire, their passion. Their wealth and lack of persecution (implicit in the "I am rich, I have prospered, and I need nothing" section) allowed them to grow lukewarm. I heard a story once of an Iranian couple who escaped to the U.S. because of the persecution that they were facing. Within a year, the wife told her husband that they needed to go back. She could feel her faith falling asleep as she remained in the U.S. So, back to persecution they went. Religious freedom is a quiet croon that lulls us into sleep. If we are not careful, we become lukewarm and sleepy Christians. Because of the Laodiceans' lukewarmness, Jesus said to them, "I will spit you out of my mouth." It is a good warning to us as well.

So What?

Religious freedom is one of the most dangerous things that Christians can face. As noted above, religious freedom often makes sleepy (lukewarm) Christians. How common is it for a Christian in America to be content with just going to church on Sunday and maybe a Wednesday small group? It is *extremely* common. This is a direct result of both religious freedom and the pursuit of happiness. There is no urgency to spread the gospel. And why would we be urgent in this? It is ingrained into us that everyone should be free to choose what they want to believe. While that is a true statement, it is in direct conflict with the knowledge that anyone who doesn't believe in Christ will *perish*. There are many Christians who are content with not spreading the gospel for the simple reason that our culture has made it clear that you are free to believe whatever you want. If you look at other countries that have strong persecution (like Iran or China), you see a different type of Christianity than is normally shown here. They are constantly putting their lives on the line to spread the gospel and to live for Christ. Why is that? I believe that this mainly comes from the fact that there are *no* wishy-washy Christians in these countries. You know what you are getting into when you become a disciple of Christ in those countries. You simply *know* that you will likely die—or at least be beaten and imprisoned—for your faith. This makes Christians in these countries very active in living out their faith. They know, from day one, that choosing to follow Christ is the most costly thing on the planet. This is *not* the normal conversion story in America. How often do we see people choose to follow Christ, but then nothing really changes in their lives? Unfortunately, it is the norm. It was true for me as well. However, I was worse than that. I made an outward appearance of choosing to follow Christ but had *zero* heart change. Playing that game in China simply wouldn't fly.

We don't have to fear anything in the USA at this point, although I expect that to change in the near future. Right now, all we have to fear is people thinking that we are idiots for believing in God. Thus, we have no reason to truly look at our faith and question whether it is worth dying for. I suggest anyone who reads this takes the time to really consider if you would die for your faith. Don't just flippantly say yes to that question. Think hard about it. I believe that if we will dwell on the fact that Christ calls us to follow even to the point of death, and we can truly say, "Yes, Jesus, I will follow you to the end no matter the cost" then we will truly live for him. For example, when I was in the military, we trained regularly. We would replay scenarios *over* and *over* both in thinking and in practice. This constant revisiting of our training is what ingrained it into our minds. Thus, when crap hits the fan, our muscles and minds will automatically know what to do. Likewise, if we truly understand what being a Christian could cost us and have truly decided that it is worth the cost, then we will follow Christ wholeheartedly, even to death. That said, I also believe that if the Christians in America wake up and truly start following Christ, the persecution will come. We are not persecuted because we don't truly follow Christ and are not a threat; however, the second that changes, we will become a real threat to Satan. People always talk about how great our country would be if the Christians truly followed Christ, and while that would be a truly glorious day, I don't think our country would become great from it. Luckily, it has nothing to do with making the United States great. Rather, it has everything to do with winning souls for the kingdom of God and teaching them to do the same.

Chapter Ten

Scientific Naturalism v Creationism

Both scientific naturalism and biblical creationism claim to know the truth of the origins of the universe. Each one uses different methods to determine this truth (i.e., creationism claims that biblical revelation is the key to the distant past, while naturalism claims that observing nature is the key). Reality does not allow for both worldviews to be accurate. Thus, we must ask: Which worldview has the better method? The scientific method is the lens through which scientific naturalism filters all data, whereas biblical revelation is the lens through which biblical creationism filters all data. This chapter demonstrates that, unlike biblical revelation, the scientific method is ineffectual in answering questions regarding the universe's origin.

Analysis of Scientific Naturalism

To begin with, it is imperative to look at the major beliefs of scientific naturalism and how those who hold to this worldview use the scientific method in cosmology, geology, biology, and anthropology when discussing origins. The mainstream view in all these scientific fields is scientific naturalism. That said, not all scientists in these fields are scientific naturalists.

The first thing that should be looked at is the explanation of how the universe itself came into being. Scientific naturalism holds that the Big Bang was the start of the universe as we know it. According to scientists who hold this view, the Big Bang happened roughly 13.8 billion years ago. How this actually played out is up for debate, but it is generally accepted that 1. The Big Bang occurred, and 2. The Big Bang happened approximately 13.8 billion years ago.

In addition to the Big Bang being the start of the universe as we know it, naturalism holds that all matter that exists today was in existence prior to the Big Bang. While this is the common view today, there are still those who suggest matter came from nothing and, in some cases, is *still* coming from nothing. Naturalism's adherents claim that matter is eternal—or, if they don't use that term, they insist that matter has always existed in some form. Additionally, very few contemporary scientists claim matter came from nothing.

One of the major tenets of scientific naturalism (and the source of the name) is the belief that all things, both living and non-living, came about by natural processes, by chance, over billions of years. There was no designer. There is no God. There is absolutely *nothing* outside of nature. Nature itself, whether biotic or abiotic, evolved on its own and by chance. In his video series *Cosmos: A Personal Journey*, Carl Sagan made this statement: "The Cosmos is all that is or was or ever will be."[1] This is exactly what scientific naturalists as a whole believe. Everything that has ever existed or will ever exist is natural. This precludes any kind of supernatural being or thing.

---

1. Carl Sagan et al., *Cosmos: A Personal Journey* (Studio City, CA: Cosmos Studies), 2000.

Finally, scientific naturalism holds the scientific method as supreme. If something cannot be known through reason and the scientific method, then it is not real. Additionally, the scientific method is viewed as effective for determining the origins of the universe and everything in it. Each area of science that tries to answer questions on the origins of something, whether that is the earth, life, or the universe itself, espouses that the scientific method is the best and only method for answering them. There are a variety of ways that the scientific method is used to explain and date the matter in the universe and the universe itself. For example, scientists cut ice cores, and count the layers based on the cycle of snow-melt followed by new snow. Scientists claim that this method demonstrates at least 800,000 years (with one melt layer and one fresh snow layer indicating one summer and winter cycle), with one claim stating that ice has been drilled that dates back 2.7 million years.[2]

Critique of Scientific Naturalism

Now that an overview of the major beliefs of scientific naturalism has been addressed, it is time to dissect them to determine if they hold up to scrutiny.

The Big Bang itself is not necessarily a problem; however, the time frame (roughly 13.8 billion years ago) is based on observational science, which is ineffective for learning how things progressed before recorded history. Additionally, the claim that it all happened from natural processes is farfetched for reasons that will be addressed later. The Big Bang is not

---

2. Paul Voosen, "2.7-Million-Year-Old Ice Opens Window on Past," *Science*, August 18, 2017, https://www.science.org/doi/10.1126/science.357.6352.630.

problematic simply because it, or something like it, probably happened. The *cause* and *timeline* are in question here rather than the plausibility of the universe expanding from a single point in an instant.

One of the more common views of what happened prior to the Big Bang is that a small, infinitely dense ball of matter and energy existed which then expanded rapidly into the universe as we know it. One significant problem with this lies in the fact that this ball of matter remained in a constant state of stasis for an infinite amount of time prior to 13.8 billion years ago. Then, *something* changed and all of a sudden this ball that had been in stasis for eternity past exploded into the universe as we now know it. What changed? There is no rational explanation for this. Additionally, this begs the question, "Where did this infinitely dense ball of matter and energy come from in the first place?" Any attempt to explain it from a naturalistic point of view will run into the exact same question. While this line of questioning could literally go on for eternity if a scientific naturalist continued to give an answer to the question (as is the case with the Big Bounce theory which says the universe expands and then collapses only to immediately expand again and so on), there will always be one more "Where did that come from?" question to meet it.

Before moving on, I would like to engage with the Big Bounce theory a bit more as it seems to me to provide the most reasonable, though flawed, argument for matter existing eternally. This theory says that the force of gravity will eventually overcome the expansion of the universe and collapse everything back together, heating it back up due to the compression of all matter. At this point, the universe would then be able to re-expand in another Big Bang and we would, potentially, have another functioning universe until gravity overcame the expansion once again. While this does *not* address the question of the previous paragraph (it just pushes it further back), it does seem more reasonable that something like this has occurred for eternity rather than the traditional view of the Big Bang. That said, there are a couple of major problems with this theory. First, agnostic astrophysicist Robert Jastrow writes, "The facts indicate the Universe will expand forever."[3] Basically, based on the current expansion rate and the estimated density of the universe, the calculations demonstrate that the universe *will not stop* expanding by a factor of three.[4] Second, it has been observed that the universe is not only expanding, but it is expanding at an *increasing* rate.[5] Essentially, gravity is *not* slowing the expansion rate down, but the opposite is actually happening. Thus, even scientifically speaking, it is quite unlikely that the Big Bounce theory is true.

Now, back to the question at hand. The problem with the "Where did that come from?" question is easily seen in the laws of the universe. They, quite simply, do not allow for something to come from nothing. No matter how many years are thrown at nothing, it will never become something. The First Law of Thermodynamics states that energy cannot be created or destroyed; it can only be transferred or changed from one form to another (like a heater converting electrical energy into heat energy). The same law applies to matter. A quick example of this is the burning of wood. When the wood is burned, it seems to be destroyed. However, it is merely *changed* from the form of wood into smoke (which is a mixture of various

---

3. Jastrow, *God and the Astronomers*, 102.

4. Ibid.

5. Nathaniel Scharping, "Gravitational Waves Show How Fast the Universe Is Expanding," *Astronomy*. October 18, 2017, https://www.astronomy.com/science/gravitational-waves-show-how-fast-the-universe-is-expanding/.

compounds including but not limited to water vapor and CO_2), ash, and heat. This is precisely *why* scientific naturalists must hold to the view that matter is eternal. However, that spells disaster for scientific naturalism which has the major tenet that everything came about by natural processes. This brings up another problem: entropy.

One of the natural processes that the universe is subject to is entropy. The second law of thermodynamics states that the level of entropy (amount of disorder/randomness in a closed system) cannot decrease unless acted upon by something outside of the closed system. The universe, being a closed system, is in a constant state of entropy and never moves from disorder to order unless acted upon by an outside force. Since the claim is that there *is no outside force*, the universe could never have gone from disordered to ordered. Yet, that is precisely the claim made by naturalism. This is the fundamental idea of evolution. The claim is that order came from chaos. Entropy simply does not work like that.

Another major problem is that it is impossible for the universe to get where it is today through natural processes alone. Certain stages in evolution are impossible transitions, even when throwing billions of years at them. While there is a plethora of examples for this, only two will be looked at for the sake of space. The first example is the transition from nonliving things to living things. Evolution claims that, through random chance and over millions or billions of years, nonliving matter arranged itself perfectly to form the first organism. Not only are the odds for all the right atoms coming together perfectly to form a cell astronomical on their own, but *also* the cell had to be able to reproduce after it was formed. Otherwise, the cell would simply die, and the whole process would need to start over. In other words, the first bacteria would necessarily have to have been a perfectly functioning bacteria for any of this process to work. The second example is very similar to the first. The transition from single-celled, asexual bacteria to multi-celled, sexual creatures is impossible. The idea is that a single-celled bacteria would evolve over millions or billions of years to become a sexual creature. *However*, this time there needs to be *two* of them at the same place and same time, *and* they need to be of the opposite sex! The odds of the first example are astronomical, but the odds of this example happening are significantly worse.

Finally, the scientific method is what scientific naturalists use to explain the age and origins of the universe and earth. The problem is that applying the scientific method to events that happened in the past requires an assumption that things happened in the exact same way as they do today. For example, a scientific naturalist might look at a particular layer of sedimentary rock and measure its thickness. He might then observe an area where sediment layers are actively being laid and keep precise measurements of how much is added each year. From there, he will calculate how long it would take a sediment layer as thick as the original to form based solely on the rate at which sediment was actively being laid down in modern times. This answer regularly results in millions of years. The question, then, is this: Is there evidence that these events (the formation of new sedimentary layers or ice layers) happen more quickly than is suggested by the scientific method? The answer is a resounding "yes." For example, modern observations have suggested that the Arctic and Antarctic form two new layers of ice every year.[6] However, a squadron of World War II planes called "The Lost Squadron" was lost in central Greenland in 1942.

---

6. Robert M. Hazen, "How Old Is Earth, and How Do We Know?" *Evo Edu and Outreach* 3, May 26, 2010, https://evolution-outreach.biomedcentral.com/articles/10.1007/s12052-010-0226-0.

At least three of the planes have been found with one P-38 (*Glacier Girl*) being recovered in 1992. Each plane was found under at least 250 feet of ice. In his book on paleoclimatology, Raymond Bradley commented on the rate at which snow accumulates each year in Greenland as averaging ".24 m ±5% on this timescale for the last ~9000 years."[7] As is immediately clear, there is a distinct problem here. *Glacier Girl* was pulled from the ice in 1992 at a depth of 300 feet (~91 meters). At that depth, based on the snow accumulation rate alone (discounting things like compression), one would expect *Glacier Girl* to have gone down nearly four hundred years ago, not fifty (at the time it was recovered). Another example comes in the form of polystrate fossils, which are fossils that span multiple sedimentary layers. How did that happen? It could not have been over a process of millions of years.

Defense of Christianity

Scientific naturalism and the scientific method may not provide the answers to the origins of the universe, but can Christianity do any better? Does biblical revelation provide satisfactory answers where the scientific method could not?

First, a common objection needs to be addressed. The question, "Where did that come from?" is commonly used against God in the same manner as was used above against scientific naturalism. That said, God, being supernatural and thus not constrained by the laws of the universe, is the one being/thing that *can* exist throughout eternity. Anything natural,

---

7. Raymond S. Bradley, *Paleoclimatology: Reconstructing Climates of the Quaternary* (Amsterdam: Elsevier, 1999), 151.

by nature, simply *cannot* exist eternally. This is based on the logic that if matter is eternal, or if all matter sprang into existence from nothing, then it is actually supernatural in origin. Natural things must come about from nature or be created by a supernatural being. Natural things cannot spring from nothing. Natural things *devolve* into greater entropy, they do not remain stable or evolve into lesser entropy. That said, God is not limited by anything natural. This means that, unlike the universe, he does not need to have had a beginning. It is perfectly logical to say that a supernatural being has lived for all eternity while it is *illogical* for the same to be said of natural beings and objects.

Biblical revelation is more effective for answers to questions regarding origins than the scientific method. It is impossible to know what happened at the beginning of the universe unless someone was there. Scientists make up all kinds of theories about how things *could* have gone down, but they will never have an answer if they are limited to the scientific method. On the other hand, a Christian has the very words of the God who created everything. Going into a defense of the Bible being God's Word is beyond the scope of this chapter, but there is an abundance of evidence, including historically verifiable accounts that demonstrate the reliability of Scripture.

What does Scripture say regarding the universe's origins? Well, Scripture begins with, "In the beginning, God created the heavens and the earth." This is very straightforward. God created the universe. The rest of the chapter goes on to describe the six days of creation. One of the things that is said by God throughout the chapter is that the creatures he created were created "according to their kind" (Genesis 1:11, 21, and 24). Interestingly, even to this day, animals produce only animals of their own kind. For example, dogs produce more dogs, and cats produce more cats. There is variation among these kinds, but there is no evidence from the fossil record nor any observed evidence that demonstrates one kind becoming another. The only type of evolution that has any evidence comes in the form of microevolution, basically another term for adaptation, which is changes within kinds (a German Shepherd and a Pomeranian, for example, both likely came from wolves or some similar wild dog). This is strong evidence for biblical revelation while it is highly problematic for scientific naturalism. Macroevolution (change from one kind to another) is seen as a scientific law though it only has the name of "theory." However, it does not deserve the term "scientific theory" as there is no demonstrable evidence that it has ever occurred or is still occurring. Thus, it is at best a hypothesis. Essentially, this means that scientific naturalists hold staunchly to a myth in the same way they claim creationists do. Yet the evidence supports creationism.

Scientific naturalism and creationism both have similar presuppositions. Each one believes, without the willingness to compromise, that something is true and then works to prove it. For naturalists, this presupposition is that there is only matter and energy. Everything that they do gets filtered through that lens. All data that is received must align with this. There can be no other answer. On the other hand, creationism has a presupposition that there is a being beyond matter and energy and that this being created everything. Similar to naturalism, this then is the lens through which a creationist views everything. Yet, this does not mean that a creationist cannot accept or produce objective science. In fact, the opposite is true. Christians were the original scientists and first started most of the universities that are still in operation today.[8] This makes sense because God, whom Christians worship, is a God of order. Thus, if he is a God of order, and he created everything, then it is logical that we could expect his creation to behave in a logical and orderly way. Naturalists should not expect to see *any* order in the universe because they believe that it came about by mere chance. Therefore, the fact that we have laws and constants in science is strong evidence for a Creator.

Conclusion

Despite the claim that scientific naturalism is based purely on logic and the scientific method, it is clear that naturalists are as uncompromising in their beliefs as creationists are. Unfortunately, these beliefs are founded not on the basis of evidence, but rather on the blind belief that there is no God. Logic, and even the scientific evidence that is held in such high esteem, demonstrate that the scientific method is ineffective for determining what happened at the beginning of time. Jastrow goes so far as to call this a kind of religion. He states,

> This religious faith of the scientist is violated by the discovery that the world had a beginning under conditions in which the known laws of physics are not valid, and as a product of forces or circumstances we cannot discover. When that happens, the scientist has lost control. If he really examined the implications, he would be traumatized. As usual when

---

8. Bodie Hodge, "Harvard, Yale, Princeton, Oxford—Once Christian?" *Answers Magazine*, June 27, 2007, https://answersingenesis.org/christianity/harvard-yale-princeton-oxford-once-christian/.

> faced with trauma, the mind reacts by ignoring the implication—in science this is known as "refusing to speculate"—or trivializing the origin of the world by calling it the Big Bang, as if the Universe were a firecracker.[9]

He goes on to say that science *cannot* answer the questions regarding the universe at, or before, its start. The scientific method may not be able to provide these answers; however, biblical revelation is effective at providing these answers, and the evidence supports it. I will leave you with this last quotation by Jastrow.

> For the scientist who has lived by his faith in the power of reason, the story ends like a bad dream. He has scaled the mountains of ignorance; he is about to conquer the highest peak; as he pulls himself over the final rock, he is greeted by a band of theologians who have been sitting there for centuries.[10]

---

9. Jastrow, *God and the Astronomers*, 105.

10. Ibid., 107.

Chapter Eleven

Young Earth v Old Earth Creationism

One of the more hotly debated topics in the contemporary church is the age of the earth. Some hate the topic because they see it as divisive and try to minimize discussion on it, while others devote their entire lives to defending one side. Among lay Christians, there is a tendency to ignore the debate, either because they see it as divisive or because they are ignorant of its importance. Primarily arguing from Scripture, this chapter seeks to show that the only reasonable way to interpret the biblical account of creation is from the young earth perspective.

Scripture is clear: God made the heavens and the earth and all that is in the earth. The very first chapter of the Bible drives that point home. God, and God alone, created everything. Not only that, but he did it in a personal way. At the end of each day, Scripture says that God looked at what he had made and saw that "it was good." He then personally created man and woman and gave them authority over his creation. The debate generally does not hinge on this, yet the debate *does* affect these teachings.

What, then, can be said about the debate over creation? Is there a right answer? Does it matter what we believe so long as we believe that God made everything? Because of the length of this chapter, I cannot address all the arguments that really ought to be addressed. That said, there is one argument in particular that needs to be looked at. As Christians, we recognize that God is truth, and his Word is truth. There can only be one truth statement for any given topic. That truth statement can be complex, involving multiple lines or even pages of discourse; but regardless of length, a fully accurate and truthful statement on any given topic is *the* truth on that topic. For example, the existence of gravity is a truth in our universe. There is a "gravitational constant" which is the same no matter where we are in the universe. The gravitational pull we *feel* is different depending on where we are in the universe, but the constant itself never changes. Likewise, creation theology has exactly *one* right answer. It can be used in any number of ways, but how God created the universe can only have one truth statement associated with it. Young Earth Creationism (YEC), Old Earth Creationism (OEC), progressive creationism, and the myriad of others that I didn't mention *cannot* all be legitimate. The question that must be asked then is this: What is the best method for determining which belief is legitimate? Is science the best method? While science is helpful, it cannot properly address anything from the past. Scientists must make assumptions that how things happen today is how things happened in the past. In geology, this is known as uniformitarianism. The issue is that there is no way to prove that a certain sedimentary layer took, for example, three million years to form. Tests can be run in labs, or we can observe nature, but there will always be assumptions that have to be made. And, as Mount St. Helens and other natural disasters have shown, nature can work *very* quickly to change the landscape. This is all without supernatural intervention. Ultimately, this means that science, while helpful, is not the best method for determining how old the earth is. If only we had the writings of someone who was there, then we could know how the world was made. Luckily for us, we have that. But not only do we have a witness, we have the Creator himself telling us what he did. God made the heavens and the earth, and he told us how he did it. This makes a literal reading of Scripture the best method for determining how God created the heavens and the earth. YEC is the only method that takes Genesis 1–11 at its word.

History and Contemporary Debates Regarding Creation

The history of creation theology is one of relative stagnancy until roughly the mid-seventeenth century. Del Ratzsch notes,

> Historically, most people (including scientists) have believed that there was an active mind (or minds) behind the visible face of nature and that some (or all) visible things and events were results of and thus evidence of the intentions and activity of that mind (minds). Nature, as most saw it, was deliberately *planned, directed,* or *designed*.[1]

As noted, this belief began to change in the mid-seventeenth century. During this time men began to view the earth as old. To be sure, some people and cultures viewed the earth as very old or even eternal prior to this. For example, Aristotle believed that "the Earth had always existed and was in an almost eternal state."[2] But it wasn't until the seventeenth and eighteenth centuries that people started to try to find evidence from the

---

1. Del Ratzsch *Science and Its Limits: The Natural Sciences in Christian Perspective* (Downers Grove, IL: InterVarsity Press, 2009), 111.

2. Dylan Campbell, "Aristotle's On the Heavens." *World History Encyclopedia*, October 16, 2016, https://www.worldhistory.org/article/959/aristotles-on-the-heavens/.

earth itself about its age. As science started to "prove" that the earth is old, many theologians began to reinterpret passages of Scripture to align with contemporary science. Up until this point, a literal reading of Genesis was the norm. Now, on the one side, we have those who hold to a literal reading of Genesis which precludes an old earth but isn't necessarily anti-science. On the other side, we have those who trust the science and believe that Scripture must align with it. Those who trust in the science over a literal reading of Genesis tend to have much more variety in what they believe than those who take a literal view of Genesis.

Young Earth Creationism, which is sometimes called biblical creationism, is primarily concerned with what the Bible says about creation. It does so by viewing Genesis as being a literal historical account of how God created the universe. In YEC, science can be and is used to back up Scripture but should never contradict Scripture. There are many legitimate scientists who hold to this view of creation despite it being counter to mainstream science. One of the primary concerns for a young earth creationist is what happens when we take creation, and more broadly Genesis 1–11, as being non-literal. Old Testament professor Kyle Dunham says, "Each category of systematic theology, to one degree or another, touches on the core tenet of God as Creator and of humankind as his consummative, image-bearing creature."[3] The foundation of most, if not all, major doctrines of Christianity is found in the beginning of Genesis. The argument is this: If we view Genesis 1–11 as allegorical then we lose the foundation for many of our doctrines, and the gospel itself is under attack. Thus, a young earth creationist will staunchly hold to a literal interpretation of the first eleven chapters of Genesis.

Old Earth Creationism is essentially the view that God created everything; however, instead of asserting that Genesis 1 is a literal six-day account of creation, it applies some level of allegory to it. The general concern of old earth creationists is the alienation of the scientific world. On this, Dr. Denis Lamoureux says, "The greatest problem with young earth creation is that it completely contradicts every modern scientific discipline that investigates the origins of the universe and life. There are very few scientists working in the disciplines of cosmology, geology, and biology who accept this anti-evolutionary position."[4] While many view OEC as its own view of creation, I would argue that OEC is the umbrella term for every view other than YEC. Each of the other views ascribes to the belief that the earth is far older than a young earth creationist allows. An old earth is the common theme between them all. For example, a strict old earth creationist would say that God created everything exactly as it is written in Genesis 1; however, he did it millions, if not billions, of years ago based on the view that the Hebrew word *yom* can mean a longer period of time than a single day. While the word can be and is used for longer time frames, the day and night phrasing in the creation account in Genesis 1 doesn't allow for these other meanings.

The above discussion of OEC is what I would call "pure" old earth creationism. Any of the other views of creation also apply the old earth model; however, they are not as pure. The view of evolution is primarily what changes. A strict old earth creationist wouldn't view evolution, at least macroevolution, as true. The same can be said of progressive creationism. But, when we get to the theistic or deistic evolution theories, evolution comes into play in a major way. These theories not only support the secular scientific view of a 4.5-billion-year-old earth, but also support

---

4. Denis O. Lamoureux, *I Love Jesus & I Accept Evolution* (Eugene, OR: Wipf and Stock Publishers, 2009), 22.

macroevolution as it is taught in the secular world. Really the only difference between these views and secular science is they believe that God initiated macroevolution rather than everything coming from nothing.

Arguments Against Young Earth Creationism

To begin with, I want to engage with some of the major arguments *against* YEC. This is not exhaustive by any means, but it does address the common arguments against YEC.

"Yom" Can Mean More than Twenty-four Hours

Old Earth Creationism focuses on the first few chapters of Genesis as saying that each "day" of creation was millions if not billions of years.[5] The argument is essentially that "yom," the Hebrew word for "day" can be translated two different ways. There is the literal twenty-four-hour period, and then there is an age of time. It can be used exactly like we use "day" in English. For example, "in the day of King David" isn't talking about a literal use of the word "day." It is talking about the period of the kingship of David which was many years. The OEC argument stems directly from the use of "day" in Genesis chapter two. "These are the generations of the heavens and the earth when they were created, in the *day* that the Lord God made the earth and the heavens" (Genesis 2:4, emphasis added). So far so good, right? This "day" indeed refers to a period of time greater than a twenty-four-hour day. That being said, six days is indeed longer than twenty-four hours. So now we must go back to Genesis 1. How is "day" used then? Genesis 1:5 says,

---

5. An even more fundamental OEC view is the "gap theory" which essentially argues that millions or billions of years occurred between Genesis 1:1 and 1:2 (or 1:2 and 1:3). Many do not hold to this view.

God called the light Day, and the darkness he called Night. And there was *evening and there was morning*, the first day (emphasis mine).

This is repeated all the way through the creation story. Using evening and morning like that is a clear statement of what God is saying. The context of the text doesn't allow for the massive amounts of time that OE creationists want to make it say. OEC says that this is up for interpretation. This is very dangerous because the Bible is not up for interpretation, at least not in the way that they mean. It doesn't mean what we want it to mean, but rather, it means exactly what God wants it to mean. If the passage is clear, we need to treat it as such. God using "evening and morning" when discussing a "day" is about as clear as you can get. Like in English, *yom* can only mean a period of time greater than twenty-four hours *if and only if* the context allows for it. Saying, "Man, my day sucked" *does not mean*, "Man, my age sucked" or "Man, my week sucked." The context just doesn't allow for it. However, saying, "Back in my day" indicates a greater period of time than a single day. One of the things drilled into your head when you go to Bible school or seminary (at least it should be) is "context is king."[6] We interpret the Scriptures through context. The context of this passage dictates that it is a literal six-day period. This is especially true when we look at the creation of light and its separation form darkness in Genesis

---

6. Many hermeneutics writers and professors like to take the "location, location, location" rule from real estate and apply it to hermeneutics by saying the "rule" of hermeneutics is "context, context, context." This is a good way of emphasizing just how important context is for correctly interpretating Scripture or any other document.

1:4–5. In this passage, "day" is clearly noted to be the time in which it is light while "night" is clearly noted to be the time of darkness.

Another huge problem that comes up with this argument is that it calls God a liar right to his face. Exodus specifically says that God created everything in six days, and on the seventh, he rested. In Exodus 20:1, the text says that God literally spoke out loud when he gave Moses the ten commandments. In verse 11, God says,

> For in *six days* Yahweh made heaven and earth, the sea, and all that is in them, and rested on the *seventh day*. Therefore Yahweh blessed the *Sabbath day* and made it holy (emphasis added).

God himself said this, so OEC is calling God a liar directly.

Unfortunately, many YE creationists do not help much on this point. It is often asked: If the earth is young, why do the earth and universe seem so old? The answer that many YE creationists give to that is that God made it with the *appearance* of age. The immediate and obvious response to that is: That makes God a deceiver. OE creationists point this out correctly. If God made everything with the appearance of age specifically to fool us, then he *is* a deceiver. Both sides of the argument are forgetting something very crucial. God made everything just as he wanted it, not in any attempt to deceive. Let me ask you this: At what stage of life were Adam and Eve created? Were they created as babies, adolescents, or adults? According to Scripture, they were created as adults. If you had taken a guess at their age the moment that they were created, you would have guessed that they were maybe twenty or thirty years old, yet they weren't even a day old! God made them as the *complete* image of what he wanted. He made the rest of creation: the earth, the sun, the moon, the creatures of the earth, and the universe in the exact same way, not trying to deceive us but rather because that was just how he wanted them. As a side note, this is also why I find the whole debate over whether the chicken or the egg came first to be ridiculous. If Scripture is true, and I believe it is, the answer is *clearly* that the chicken came first. This is only a challenging question to those who do not hold to biblical revelation.

Additionally, in contrast to the way a lot of lay Christians respond to the question about appearance, more informed YE creationists argue that the earth and universe only "appear" old because of the paradigm that one approaches the question with. Basically, the average person today *assumes* the earth is old because that is what we have been told by scientists who also assume that the processes we see today have remained unchanged in the past. This is known as uniformitarian geology and is the common way geology is treated today. Creation scientists and philosophers take the same evidence secular scientists and philosophers take, but we interpret the evidence in light of the historically accurate document commonly known as the Bible. For example, though not a biblical literalist, renowned archaeologist Nelson Glueck writes,

> As a matter of fact, however, it may be stated categorically that no archaeological discovery has ever controverted a Biblical reference. Scores of archaeological findings have been made which confirm in clear outline or in exact detail historical statements in the Bible. And, by the same token, proper evaluation of Biblical descriptions has often led to amazing

discoveries. They form tesserae in the vast mosaic of the Bible's almost incredibly correct historical memory.[7]

Basically, a Christian scientist can look at the evidence, like the Grand Canyon, and see evidence of a *young* earth. Some examples that point to a young earth from the Grand Canyon are the layers of earth that are virtually flat and show little to no evidence of erosion between them, the fact that the whole Grand Canyon does not actually follow the path of the Colorado River (and thus cannot have been carved by it), and that the same layers found in the Grand Canyon can be found across the USA and even on other continents. These better point to a catastrophic, global flood creating the layers and then a lake or sea rapidly draining to cut the Grand Canyon than they do to a million or billion-year-plus set of processes. Ultimately, what may *appear* to be old does not necessarily *have* to be old. One's paradigm can easily produce two very different results when looking at the same bits of evidence.

A couple of paragraphs ago, I brought up the universe as a whole as part of the "appearance of age" issue. This presents another problem, though I would suggest that the answer is similar in nature to the paragraph where it was first mentioned. The question is this: If the universe is young, along with the earth, then how do we see stars that are millions or billions of light years away? Shouldn't we only see stars within roughly six thousand light years? I believe that there are two possible answers to this. One aligns

---

7. Nelson Glueck, *Rivers in the Desert: A History of the Negev* (New York: Grove Press, 1959), 31. In *every* case, archeological discoveries have proven the Bible true, even when most everyone assumed the Bible was making something up. No historical evidence has been found to disprove the Bible's historical validity.

with the science of the Big Bang theory quite well, while the other is based solely on the power of God. To begin, I will address the latter. The idea here is that God, being all-powerful, simply made the light from the stars in the universe reach earth. I do believe that God absolutely could have done this. That said, I find the other method more likely. If God were to have flung the universe out from a center point (like the Big Bang theory suggests) then the light from even the most remote stars would be visible at every point in the universe *immediately*. This is simply because the light was already there. Of course, this possibility assumes that the universe was created in its current state as the Bible claims. In the case of the Big Bang theory, this would not work because it took time for stars to form after the Big Bang took place. As such, enough time would have to then pass for light to make it from one object to another.

Another thing to notice is how the Genesis story uses "night." *Laila* is the word used for "night" in Hebrew, and it always refers to the time between sunset and sunrise. Therefore, regardless of the difficulty of knowing whether "day" means twenty-four hours or an age, we can safely declare that the uses in Genesis 1 are literal twenty-four-hour days due to the repeated use of "night."

It Alienates Scientists from the Gospel

One of the biggest arguments for OEC, and arguably the one that originated the idea, is that it helps reconcile science and the Bible. The argument is essentially that in order for us to minister to the scientists, we must accept science. In other words, the Bible must back up science. Conversely, if we uphold Scripture *above* the contemporary treatment of science, the argument goes that we will alienate the scientists. Afterall, we need to make the gospel more palatable to our audience, right? Isn't that what Paul did with the "unknown god" the Greeks were worshiping in Athens?

One common example used by old earth creationists is that Genesis 1 has God creating vegetation before creating the sun. Their question is: How can vegetation live without the sun? This is actually pretty simple. Let's first look at an earlier example of this same problem. God made day and night without the sun and the moon, which means that the sun and the moon are not needed for light. God made them to govern the day and the night, but the day and night were there before the sun and moon existed. This means that the original source of light was *God himself*. In fact, one of the biggest inclusio's in the Bible revolves around this idea of God being light.[8] Revelation 21:23–24 says,

> And the city has no need of sun or moon to shine on it, for the glory of God gives it light, and its lamp is the Lamb. By its light will the nations walk, and the kings of the earth will bring their glory into it.

So if God himself is light and he made the sun and the moon to merely govern the day and night, then there is no need to have the sun for the plants to live. God provides for them by being light himself. The greatest

---

8. An inclusio is a way ancient writers, especially in Scripture, would bracket a section of writing to signify everything in that section is connected. This typically happens within chapters or books themselves. For example, 1 Corinthians 8 begins an inclusio on food sacrificed to idols and this is closed in chapter 10. However, in the case of Genesis and Revelation, this happens quite a bit across the entirety of Scripture. It is one of the reasons I believe the canon of Scripture is closed. The brackets that opened at the beginning in Genesis are closed beautifully at the end of Revelation.

thing that should be taken away from this is that the Bible does not have to follow science. The reason for this is that God is outside of science. Don't get me wrong, science is a great thing; however, we must remember that God *created* science. God does not have to follow the laws of science because there were no laws of science until God created them. In fact, when has God ever obeyed the laws of science? There are countless acts throughout the Bible that prove that God is *not* bound by science.

The Bible Is Not a Scientific Document

The third major argument is that the Bible is not primarily a historical or scientific document. In some sense, that is true. The Bible is full of different genres, some of which are to be taken literally, while some are poetic and not to be taken literally. However, the areas treated as historical by the authors are to be treated as such by us. Instead of trying to come up with a decent argument for how certain claims in Scripture could have played out, adherents to the view that the Bible is not primarily a scientific or historical document incorrectly treat certain parts as allegorical. The problem is that this ends up creating a Bible that is *far* from inerrant or infallible. Anything considered suspect by secular science must then be discarded. This includes miracles and even God himself. It is interesting to note that, despite the fact that all archaeological evidence has proven the Bible true over and over again, secular scientists, historians, and archaeologists still treat it as an unreliable witness. It is assumed to be wrong until proven correct, and when it is proven correct, it's brushed under the table. Why on earth would *any* Christian want to be a partner in that? It's the opposite of how we treat criminal suspects. They are innocent until proven guilty. Christians should likewise approach Scripture as correct until proven wrong. If it is truly God's Word like we say it is, then it will not be proven wrong. The Bible is God's inspired Word. It is never outdated, and he doesn't make mistakes. God did not inspire the book of Genesis to be written for only one group of people at a specific point in our scientific experimenting (which means basically none). This would be a mistake. God inspired the Scriptures to be meaningful to the entire world at any point in time.

Arguments for Young Earth Creationism

The arguments against YEC are varied, and there are some valid critiques, yet they do not seem to successfully refute the biblical doctrine of creation. Now let's look at some arguments for YEC.

Genesis 1–11 Is the Foundation of Most Doctrines

The account in the first eleven chapters of Genesis is the foundation for most, if not all, of the major doctrines within our faith. By turning it into an allegory, we undermine the foundation of so many doctrines. This undermining allows for all kinds of false teachings to spring up. Let's take the attack on marriage between a man and a woman as an example. Genesis 1 teaches that God made men and women in his image and that the man would "leave his father and mother and hold fast to his wife, and they shall become one flesh." By holding that Genesis 1 is an allegory, the biblical teaching on marriage is threatened. Jesus, however, did not treat this as an allegory that can be disregarded. He said,

> Have you not read that he who created them from the beginning made them male and female, and said, "Therefore a man shall leave his father and his mother and hold fast to his wife, and the two shall become one flesh"? So they are no longer

two but one flesh. What therefore God has joined together,
let not man separate (Matthew 19:4–6).

In this passage, Jesus demonstrates a high view of creation in Genesis and uses Genesis to uphold the biblical doctrine on marriage and does so by taking a literal view of the passage.

It Holds Scripture as Supreme

If God is truly the author of Scripture and it is true that he cannot lie or say or do anything wrong or evil, then Scripture is the gold standard for how we should view life. YEC views Scripture in this way. As such, YEC holds Scripture above *everything* else. God's Word is the standard by which we should view the world and the universe. Our subjective experiences while living on this earth, even if said experiences follow the scientific method, are not as reliable as God's own Word. I won't rehash the previous chapter here. Instead, I will end this section by saying this: Only God knows what happened when he created the world and Scripture claims to be God's Word to us; therefore, Scripture is and should be our supreme way of knowing what happened at the beginning of time. YEC correctly holds this view while all other views do not.

Scripture Itself Is Relatively Young

Another deeply important argument to look at is the fact that we have only had Scripture for somewhere between 3,500 and 4,000 years. Additionally, it was during this time that the Messiah came to earth to reconcile the world to himself. If one is to believe the old earth idea that the universe is millions or even billions of years old, one has to be okay with the idea that God allowed suffering and death for all of that time and only decided to do something about it in the last four thousand years. This directly attacks the character of God. My God, the God of the Bible, would never do such a thing. He loves his creation far too much to subject it to that kind of torture and suffering. He would never leave his people to fend for themselves for millions of years, yet that is exactly what happens in *any* form of old earth theory, even the more conservative ones.

But, if that is true, how could God have allowed 1,500 to 2,000 years to go by with no Bible if YEC is correct? There is a relatively simple answer to this. Knowledge of God would have been passed down from father to child. Of course, this is not a perfect method. Otherwise, we never would have received God's written Word. That said, it would have been a perfectly serviceable way for this initial two thousand or so years. Additionally, taking Genesis 1 through 11 at its word, we can see that life spans were much longer and started, twice, with a single, godly family. This means that, for over nine hundred years, one could go and talk to Adam and Eve, the very people who walked in the Garden of Eden with God. It is only when these life spans become drastically shorter and a significant distance is obtained from Noah that Scripture began being written down. That said, two thousand years of no written word from God, especially in these circumstances, is in no way similar to hundreds of thousands or millions of years of silence on God's part.

Conclusion

In the end, the only reasonable way to treat Genesis 1–11 is as a literal, historical account. Any other view necessarily attacks God's Word and the vast majority of the doctrines taught throughout the rest of Scripture. Thus, YEC is the only reasonable view for Christians to hold. This does not mean that we ought to reject science. On the contrary, YE creationists have ample reason to pursue scientific discoveries. Science is a good thing and is highly valuable. It just needs to be in its proper place—below Scripture.

Chapter Twelve

Sons of God

Many Christians struggle with who the sons of God are in Genesis 6 and other similar passages. The theories range from gods to angels, fallen angels, Sethites, and watchers, among others. That said, Scripture itself does a good job of giving us a solid answer to this difficult question. I would argue that most treat this topic much too narrowly to get a good view of what God shows us through Scripture. Thus, this chapter is focused on taking a broad look at the sons of God. Who comes out on top of the pack when engaging this topic from a biblical theology standpoint?

Before I begin, let me make a note of something. *A lot* of ink has been spilled on this topic. I am one writer in a long line of people who go back thousands of years. For the most part, I am avoiding engaging too much with all of this as it would make for a much longer chapter. Instead, I am approaching this topic from a primarily scriptural standpoint. What does God's Word say about who the sons of God are? That question is the defining characteristic of this chapter. As such, do not expect a whole lot of citations, except from Scripture.

The first mention of the sons of God is in Genesis 6:2, but before we look there, let us look at what the New Testament has to say on this matter. Aside from the fact that, as Christians, we are all adopted with full rights as sons and daughters of God, there is a verse that clarifies who the Old Testament sons of God were. "Kenan was the son of Enosh. Enosh was the son of Seth. Seth was the son of Adam. Adam was the *son of God*" (Luke 3:38, emphasis added). So, Adam is the son of God. More importantly, that sonship continued through the line that God chose, which means that it was not the angels who were labeled the sons of God in Genesis. This brings us to Genesis 6:2. This is a difficult verse, but one that I think has a solid explanation. "The sons of God saw the beautiful daughters of men and took any they wanted as their wives" (Genesis 6:2). Thus, we got the Nephilim. Maybe. The passage does not specify that the Nephilim are the children of the union between the sons of God and daughters of men. It connects the timing for sure but, beyond that, we do not know much. It is erroneous to assume that the union between the sons of God and the daughters of men resulted in the Nephilim. Scripture only says, "The Nephilim were on the earth in those days, and also afterward, when the sons of God came in to the daughters of man they bore children to them" (Genesis 6:4). It *does not* directly connect the Nephilim with the children of this unholy union. We would do well to remember that fact.

Now many people think that the sons of God are angels or maybe demons in this verse, but there are several reasons to argue that they aren't. First, God only punishes man in Genesis 6. If the angels, demons, or something else were involved in the events of Genesis 6, then God would have punished them just as he punished Adam, Eve, and Satan in the garden. All guilty parties would be punished. Only humans are punished; therefore, only humans were involved in the deeds. Additionally, the context of Genesis 6 only involves man's sin. In his commentary on 1 Peter, Wayne Grudem notes,

> Though there are different views on whether Genesis 6:1–4 refers to the sin of angels when it talks about the "sons of God"... there can be no dispute that the entire section immediately preceding the command to build the ark (Gen. 6:5–13) clearly emphasizes human sin, and human sin alone, as the reason God brings the flood upon the earth. God is not sorry that he has made angels, but that he made man (v. 6). He does not decide to blot out fallen angels, but man (vv. 6, 13); it is not the violence and corruption of angels which arouses his anger, but the violence and corruption of man (vv. 5, 11, 12, 13).[1]

Basically, only human sin is in view prior to the destruction of the world. If the view that the sons of God in Genesis 6 are fallen angels is correct, why then does God not address said fallen angels or their sin in the chapter? God only addresses mankind and their sin as a reason for destroying the earth, and this is significant.

Second, the verses immediately prior talk about the sons of God, starting with Adam, whom we have already noted is God's son, on down through Noah. It is important to note that this lineage doesn't include Cain. It is also important to look at the verse that starts the lineage, "This is the book of the generations of Adam. When God created man, he created them in the likeness of God" (Genesis 5:1). "Likeness of God" goes back to Genesis 1:26. In fact, Seth is said to have been fathered by Adam "in his own likeness, after his image" (Genesis 5:3) just as Adam was "fathered"

---

1. Wayne Grudem, *1 Peter: An Introduction and Commentary* (Downers Grove, IL: InterVarsity Press, 1988), 224.

by God, after his likeness, and in his image. The best way to understand this is that Seth could rightly be called a "son of God" in the same way that Luke 3:38 records Adam as being the "son of God." Why Seth and not Cain? This is simple. Seth, and the descendants after him, were godly while Cain and his descendants were not. In other words, they bore the image of God well while Cain and his descendants squandered the image of God. The entirety of Genesis 5 is devoted to laying out this godly line all the way down through to Noah. This line is also in direct contrast to Genesis 4 which is focused on Cain's ungodliness and the ungodliness of his descendants. Then, in Genesis 6, we immediately move into a discussion of the sons of God and the daughters of men. As such, the line of Seth (the sons of God or those who followed God) was marrying into the line of Cain (daughters of men or godless women). I am not saying that the Sethites were *all* sons of God. The only people that qualify as sons of God are those who follow God. What I *am* saying is that, generally speaking, the line of Seth *were* the ones who followed God. This is very different than angels marrying human women. When the Law of Moses is given, there are very strict instructions against marrying outside of the Israelites. Furthermore, there are commands in the New Testament against believers marrying nonbelievers. Obviously, this is something that God really doesn't want us to do. He gives us the reason as well. Deuteronomy 7:3–4 says,

> You shall not intermarry with them, giving your daughters to their sons or taking their daughters for your sons, for they would turn away your sons from following me, to serve other gods. Then the anger of Yahweh will be kindled against you, and he would destroy you quickly.

That sounds quite a bit like what happened in Genesis 6, does it not? The sons of God were led away from God by the daughters of men into greater and greater disobedience against God. Then the anger of Yahweh was kindled against them and he destroyed them all, save the one who remained righteous, Noah.

Thirdly, God created animals that produce more of their own kind. "Then God said, 'Let the earth produce every sort of animal, each producing offspring of the same kind'" (Genesis 1:24). This means that angels or demons could not successfully have children with humans because those children would be half-man half-angel. Angels have no DNA to pass along to human women. Lastly, angels are either incapable or have no desire for sex. Jesus talks about this in the Synoptic Gospels. In a response to the Sadducees trying to trick Jesus regarding the resurrection, he says,

> Is this not the reason you are wrong, because you know neither the Scriptures nor the power of God? For when they rise from the dead, they neither marry nor are given in marriage, but are like angels in heaven (Mark 12:24–25).

So angels do not marry which means literally that the events of Genesis 6:2 couldn't have involved angels in that way.

Before we go any further, I want to show you all of the biblical references to the children of God. The column on the left refers to humans being called the sons or children of God. The middle column refers to Jesus being called the Son of God, and the last column refers to any ambiguous references to sons or children of God that require much more effort to understand who is being labeled as children of God.

SONS OF GOD

Humans	Jesus	Ambiguous References
Exodus 4:22	2 Samuel 7:14	Genesis 6:2
Exodus 4:23	Psalm 2:7	Genesis 6:4
Deuteronomy 8:5	Psalm 2:11–12	Job 1:6
Deuteronomy 14:1	Proverbs 30:4	Job 2:1
1 Chronicles 22:10	1 Chronicles 22:10	Job 38:7—most ambiguous
Jeremiah 31:20	Isaiah 7:14	
Malachi 1:6	Isaiah 9:6–7	
Malachi 3:16,17	Daniel 3:25	
Jeremiah 3:4	Hosea 11:1	
Jeremiah 3:19	Psalm 89:26	
Hosea 1:10		
Deuteronomy 32:6		
Deuteronomy 32:8		
Jeremiah 31:9		
Jeremiah 31:22		
Psalm 73:15		
Hosea 11:1		
Hosea 11:10		
Psalm 82—as shown in John 10:34–36		
Proverbs 3:11–12		
Psalm 68:5–6		
Isaiah 63:8		
Isaiah 63:16		
Isaiah 64:8		
New Testament References		
Humans	Jesus	Ambiguous
Matthew 5:9	Matthew 1:20	
Matthew 5:45	Matthew 2:15	
Matthew 7:9–11	Matthew 3:17	
Matthew 13:38	Matthew 4:3	
Matthew 17:26	Matthew 4:6	
Luke 6:35	Matthew 8:29	
Luke 11:11–13	Matthew 11:27	
Luke 15:11–31	Matthew 14:33	
Luke 20:36	Matthew 16:16	
John 8:39–47	Matthew 17:5	
John 10:25–38	Matthew 21:37	
John 12:36	Matthew 22:42–45	
Romans 8:14	Matthew 26:63–64	
Romans 8:19	Matthew 27:54	
Romans 8:29	Mark 1:11	
Romans 9:26	Mark 3:11	
2 Corinthians 6:18	Mark 5:7	
Galatians 3:26	Mark 9:7	
Galatians 4:6	Mark 12:6	
Galatians 4:7	Mark 12:35–37	
Hebrews 2:10	Mark 14:61–62	
Hebrews 12:5–8	Mark 15:39	
Revelation 21:7	Luke 1:35	
Romans 8:15	Luke 3:22	
Romans 8:23	Luke 4:3	
Romans 9:4	Luke 4:9	
Ephesians 1:5	Luke 4:41	
References to "your" or "our" Father	Luke 8:28	
Matthew 5:16	Luke 9:35	
Matthew 5:48	Luke 10:22	
Matthew 6:1	Luke 20:13	
Matthew 6:4–9	Luke 22:70	
Matthew 6:14–32	John 1:49	
Matthew 10:20	John 3:16–18	
Matthew 10:29	John 3:36	
Matthew 12:50	John 5:19–26	
Matthew 13:43	John 6:40	
Matthew 18:14	John 10:25–38	
Matthew 23:9	John 11:4	
Mark 11:25	John 11:27	
Luke 6:36	John 17:1	
Luke 11:2	John 20:31	
Luke 11:13	Acts 9:20	
Luke 12:30	Acts 13:33	
John 4:21–23	Romans 1:3–4	
John 14:24	Romans 1:9	
and so many more	and so many more	

See what I'm getting at here? The entire Bible says righteous *men* (humans) are God's children. I will explain the five ambiguous references further down in this chapter.

At this point, I am going to go off the beaten path briefly to try to explain the Nephilim. We don't know what "Nephilim" means; however, it is similar to the Hebrew word meaning "to fall." The Nephilim were called "heroes of old, men of renown." Additionally, they appeared to be giants. We don't see that anywhere in Genesis, but Numbers calls them giants.[2] Let's first look at their apparent size. Genesis says nothing about them being giants, only that they were "mighty men who were of old, the men of renown" (Genesis 6:4). Numbers does call them giants, but the Nephilim talked about in Numbers are in no way related to the Nephilim of Genesis because only Noah and his family survived the flood. In fact, I do not believe that the Nephilim were ever seen after the flood. Before you get outraged and call me a heretic, let me show you what I mean.

Here is Numbers 13:26–33:

> And they [the spies] came to Moses and Aaron and to all the congregation of the people of Israel in the wilderness of Paran, at Kadesh. They brought back word to them and to all the congregation, and showed them the fruit of the land. And they told him, "We came to the land to which you sent us. It flows with milk and honey, and this is its fruit. However, the people who dwell in the land are strong, and the cities are fortified and very large. And besides, we saw the

---

2. Your translation or footnotes might have "giants" in Genesis 6:4 instead of "Nephilim," but this is a mistranslation based on Numbers, as will be seen shortly.

descendants of Anak there. The Amalekites dwell in the land of the Negeb. The Hittites, the Jebusites, and the Amorites dwell in the hill country. And the Canaanites dwell by the sea, and along the Jordan. But Caleb quieted the people before Moses and said, "Let us go up at once and occupy it, for we are well able to overcome it." Then the men who had gone up with him said, "We are not able to go up against the people, for they are stronger than we are." So they brought to the people of Israel **_a bad report_** of the land that they had spied out, saying, "The land, through which we have gone to spy it out, is a land that devours its inhabitants, and all the people that we saw in it are of great height. And there we saw the Nephilim (the sons of Anak, who come from the Nephilim), and we seemed to ourselves like grasshoppers, and so we seemed to them" (emphasis mine).

So first, they merely report that the people who live in the land are powerful, and the cities are fortified and very large. They say nothing about giants, but when Caleb steals a quote from Gimli in the Battle of Helm's Deep ("Oh, come on. We can take 'em!"), they change what they said to Moses and "spread among the Israelites a bad report." They said the land sucks, the Nephilim are there, and we are like grasshoppers compared to them. So, at this point, the only thing telling us that they were giants is a false report! The *only* mention of the Nephilim in the Bible post-Genesis 6 is in a misleading story told by the spies. Notice, it is not *Moses* or even Scripture that is making this claim. This is an example of Scripture including a true, historical account about someone telling a lie.[3] Based on the facts that no Nephilim could have survived the flood and the only mention of the Nephilim after the flood comes from a false report, we can safely conclude that, whatever they were, they all died in the flood. Additionally, the only place in the Bible that refers to the Nephilim as giants is found in this same false report passage.

The discussion of Nephilim brings up an interesting question: What about the Book of Enoch? Having soundly rejected Numbers 13 as evidence for the Nephilim, all of the other "evidence" of the Nephilim being half-angel and half-human comes from the Book of Enoch. It is also the only somewhat reliable source where the Nephilim are portrayed as giants. The funny thing is that the Book of Enoch says that the giants were either three hundred or three thousand ells tall. Historically, one ell measures anywhere between eighteen and forty-five inches, so that would mean the Nephilim were anywhere from 450 to 1,125 feet tall (using three hundred ells) or 4,500 to 11,250 feet tall (using three thousand ells)! Any of those numbers is utterly ridiculous. The shortest giant, according to the Book of Enoch, would be a third of the height of the Empire State Building. What would a 450-foot human look like? Well, the heads of the presidents on Mt. Rushmore are approximately sixty feet tall, whereas the average human head measures around 9.4 inches tall and the average human male is 69.3 inches tall. If you divide 69.3 inches by 9.4 inches, you get 7.37, so it would take a little more than seven heads stacked on top of each other to equal

---

3. Scripture accurately records what the spies said even though they gave a *false* statement. This is an example of how important it is to understand the genre of whatever Bible passage we are looking at. Understanding that Numbers 13 is a historical narrative clues us in on the fact that God does not endorse everything that is done in the narrative since it is merely recording what happened.

the height of the average man. Now if we take sixty feet (the approximate height of the presidents' heads) and multiply it by 7.37, we get 442 feet tall. Do you see where I am going with this? Consider the following:

1. We have no archeological evidence that anything even remotely close to that size has ever walked on this earth.

2. The tallest dinosaur ever to be discovered was sixty feet tall (and that is because of a ridiculously long neck).

3. There were supposedly two hundred angels (or "watchers," the term used in the Book of Enoch) that interbred with humans, with some of those angels having more than one child.

4. To them, the biggest dinosaur would have looked like what a chicken does to you and me. This creates a food chain problem. The amount of food that one of these giants would need to eat in a day is *enormous*. How could a fairly young earth support over two hundred creatures of this size who could likely eat one or more large dinosaurs each day?

5. Human women supposedly gave *birth* to these behemoths. I mean, come on, women struggle enough with normal-sized children. Yet, we are to believe that a 5-foot-tall woman could birth a 450- to 11,250-foot giant? This is ridiculous on so many levels. Unless someone claims, completely without the possibility of evidence, that these giants would have been normal-sized babies somehow, we can safely assume that the Nephilim were at most large men (think 8 to 10 feet tall at the most). There *is* biblical, historical, and modern evidence for men of these sizes. However,

as was previously noted, Genesis 6 gives *no* evidence to suggest that the Nephilim were giants, even in the 8 to 10 feet range.

All of this tells me that the Book of Enoch is misguided at best and downright make-believe at worst. People argue that it is Scripture or near-Scripture based on what is written about it in Jude 1:14–15 which appears to be a quote that Jude took from the Book of Enoch. The claim is that this is proof that the Book of Enoch is reliable, but that overlooks the fact that Paul mentions many sources in his writings, many of which will never be claimed to be biblical sources just because they are quoted in Scripture.[4] Paul merely uses non-scriptural writings or sayings to point out something that the Greeks have written that coincides with the Bible or to point out things that the Greeks do not understand. He is not claiming that all their writings are true. Jude is using the same idea as Paul when he quotes from the Book of Enoch. Something from this book could still be true and useful for evidence, but there are also several different areas of Scripture that back up what is written in the section of the Book of Enoch that Jude chooses to use. As a side note, we don't know that Enoch was the author, only that he is traditionally attributed to have written the Book of Enoch (hence the name). In fact, it is extremely unlikely that Enoch wrote it, since scholars date the writing to 300-200 BC. This would require Enoch to have not only come back to earth but he also would have written something against Scripture, which would be strange for someone who "walked with God" (Genesis 5:24). The man walked so well with God that God did not let him taste death. Yet this is the man who supposedly wrote something that contradicts God? Enoch didn't write the Book of Enoch.

---

4. For example, Paul quotes a Cretan poet in Titus 1:12.

That said, what happened to Enoch *does* open the door for *someone else* to write something in his name much later.

Another interesting point is that the watchers that the Book of Enoch discusses are only mentioned in one book of the Bible. In the book of Daniel, they are mentioned three times (Daniel 4:13, 17, and 23). In this book, they are shown to be holy ones of God, but in the Book of Enoch, all the watchers committed sin and were subsequently punished for their crimes. The Book of Enoch claims that there are two hundred watchers and that *all* two hundred of them were involved with the sins of Genesis 6. What that tells us is that there *are no more holy watchers*—at least according to the Book of Enoch, which you have to believe if you want to claim that the watchers are the ones who committed the sins in Genesis. In this case, we would be calling the book of Daniel false and an extra-biblical book, one with serious issues, true.

What about giants in the Bible? We have already discovered that there is no biblical evidence to support that the Nephilim were giants, at least more than can reasonably be expected today.[5] Additionally, all of the extra-biblical descriptions are ridiculous. But the Bible does talk about giants, right? That is correct to some extent. The Bible contains a lot of imagery about people being as big and strong as trees, but those always refer to the strength of their armies and walls. Goliath is regarded as a giant, but there is significant debate as to what his size actually was. Certain texts (The Dead Sea Scrolls and the Septuagint) say that his height is 6' 9" while other texts say 9' 9". Regardless of which texts we use, we get an absolute

---

5. The tallest man in recent history, Robert Wadlow (1918-1940), was 8' 11". He was a "giant" but not on the scale that is typically applied to the Nephilim of Genesis 6. He, like most other people of unusual size, had significant issues due to his height.

maximum of ten feet tall. A big man, no doubt, but we have men near that height who are alive today. Do we call them giants? Some might, but I typically would just say that they are "big dudes." However, I suppose that I make an exception for Andre the Giant. Though a 9' or 10' person is very large compared to "normal" people, it is well within the realm of realism for humans, unlike how this topic is traditionally treated.

An interesting thing to note regarding Goliath is that the average height for men in the ancient Middle East was about 5' 2" so even if Goliath was a "mere" seven feet tall, he still would have towered over the average Israelite. Additionally, Saul was (on average) head and shoulders taller than other Israelites (1 Samuel 10:23), which makes for an interesting understanding of the passage. Saul, the tallest guy in the army, arguably the most suited person to the task, wouldn't match himself against Goliath, while David, a mere boy, gladly stood up to the Philistine champion.

Scripture also mentions an Egyptian who was 7' 6" tall (1 Chronicles 11:23) and gives several other examples of "large men" without any specific measurements. Thus, the tallest the Bible ever mentions a man being is either 7' 6" (the Egyptian) or 9' 9" (Goliath). While the Bible attests to large men, there is no agreement with the Book of Enoch and similar extra-biblical texts that these men were exceedingly large giants.

Now, let's get back to the sons of God discussion. In Job, there are three instances of the sons of God, and one in Deuteronomy that seems to be ambiguous or references something other than humans. Let's quickly look at Deuteronomy 32:8 first. Most of the oldest manuscripts (The Dead Sea Scrolls and the older manuscripts of the Septuagint) use the term "sons of God" as opposed to "sons of Israel" which the Masoretic text uses. Based on this information, it is safe to assume that the correct word is *God* and not *Israel*. Additionally, in the context of Deuteronomy 32, we can only understand the sons of God as being human because the entire chapter is devoted to the relationship between God and mankind. Angels don't fit into this chapter at all. Deuteronomy 32 is only about God and his chosen people of Israel.

The second set of verses are those found in the book of Job. There are three instances where the term "sons of God" is used in Job: once in the first chapter, once in the second chapter, and once in the thirty-eighth chapter. This is where people argue that the sons of God *have* to be angels. However, the first two mentions are very different from the mention in chapter 38, so I am going to look at them first. I *know* that these first two mentions are not angels, for angels are *always* in the presence of God unless he has sent them on a mission of some sort (Matthew 18:10, Revelation 8:2, Luke 1:19, 1 Kings 22:19, etc.). Therefore, the angels have no need to "present" themselves to God.

On the other hand, men are constantly being referred to as "presenting" themselves to God (Deuteronomy 16:16 and 31:14, Joshua 24:1, 1 Samuel 10:19, etc.). All of this makes Job the outlier if we continue saying that they were angels. These two verses in Job are also the only places where it appears that Satan can be in heaven. In all other texts involving Satan, we see that he has been cast out of heaven and is only on the earth now along with the rest of the fallen angels. He is still able to communicate with God, but he has been cast out. Thus, both of these scenes happened on earth with the sons of God being godly men presenting themselves to God and Satan coming among them to accuse them.

This brings us to Job 38:7. To be completely honest, I am not entirely sure about what to make of this verse. What I do know is that if only one verse (out of a multitude of other verses) seems to claim one thing that isn't true in any of the other verses, we must use the other verses to help interpret that one verse, not the other way around. Another thing that I know is that God never calls angels his children. Hebrews 1:5–7 says,

> For to which of the angels did God ever say, "You are my son, today I have begotten you"? Or again, "I will be to him a father, and he shall be to me a son"? And again, when he brings the firstborn into the world, he says, "Let all God's angels worship him." Of the angels, he says, "He makes his angels wind and his ministers a flames of fire."

This is saying that *no* angel was *ever* called a son of God. It also says that Christ is the firstborn, which means that there are other sons of God; and if those sons of God are not angels, then they must be righteous men. That said, Job 38:7 also cannot be talking about men, since the context is the beginning of the world prior to God's creation of man. The Bible also expressly says it couldn't be angels. It is also a plural use of sons of God so it couldn't be talking about Jesus alone (though he could be one of the ones shouting for joy). Not only that, but we need to recognize that God is using a lot of imagery in Job 38, so this could also be imagery. God is the "Father of lights" as seen in James 1:17, so he could be saying that the sun, the moon, and the stars were shouting for joy in the same way that is seen in Psalm 148:3. In Proverbs 8:22–31, wisdom is also mentioned as having been there before creation and rejoicing in everything that God was doing.

On a completely different note, something we need to understand is that Job 38:7 is a direct response from God to Job demonstrating just how little wisdom, knowledge, and understanding Job has compared to God. Thus, we might never know the answer to the Job 38:7 question—at least not until we reach heaven. All I know for sure regarding Job 38:7 is that we cannot take one verse in the Bible and say it discounts what the rest of the Bible says. The rest of the Bible says that righteous men, not angels, are the sons of God.

Conclusion

Given all the above evidence, it is far more reasonable to conclude that the sons of God in Genesis 6 were men rather than gods, angels, demons, or some other type of being. Additionally, the Nephilim are not necessarily related to the union between the sons of God and the daughters of men, and the idea that they were giants does not actually have a basis in the Bible. It can be incredibly harmful to the church to uphold things that the Bible does not teach.

Chapter Thirteen

The Doctrine of Election

THE DOCTRINE OF ELECTION is an area of Christian doctrine that is very divisive. It shouldn't be though, for the Bible shows us the truth about election and I believe it is fairly clear if one is willing to truly give it a good look. I agree to a certain extent with both sides of the argument, but I ultimately fall somewhere in the middle of the two. For those of you who don't know, the two major sides are typically labeled as Calvinism and Arminianism. Calvinism seems to be the more widely held belief, or at least adherents tend to be more vocal. Essentially, in Calvinism, God chooses who gets to know him. Period. I agree with this but not in the way that Calvinists assert. On the other hand, there are those who say that *only* human free will is at play in one's salvation. This is a more extreme case of Arminianism. I also agree that free will is a major part of how we come to Christ, but it isn't the only thing. In my search for truth on this subject, I have discovered these requirements for becoming God's chosen: being called by the Father, who has elected the way to come to him—via believing in and following his Son.

So the first thing that I am going to look at is the Calvinistic argument that God chose a nation for no particular reason to be his chosen people. While it is true that God chose a specific people to be his chosen ones, he also had reason to do it. God chose Israel as his chosen people based on several factors. First, let's look at who God actually chose. God chose Abram, not Israel to begin with. Because Abram followed God when he was called, God chose Abram's descendants to be his chosen people. As such, God chose someone who could have said no but rather chose, on a human level, to follow and obey God. Thus, Abram and his descendants were blessed. Look at what God says in Genesis 22:18, "And in your offspring shall all the nations of the earth be blessed *because* you have *obeyed* my voice" (emphasis added).

Why Abram though? For that answer, we must go back to Noah. Noah cursed Ham and asked God to bless Shem and have the descendants of Ham be Shem's servants. Why did Noah ask this? He asked because Shem was a servant of the Lord (Genesis 9:26). Shem is the ancestor of Abram. God chose from a line of God-fearing people. Since they were God-fearing, when Abram was called, he responded to God. Abram was not some random dude who didn't even believe in God.

So yes, God chose Israel, but there was significantly more to it than God just saying, "You Israelites are my holy people." Also, there are many examples of non-Israelites being saved throughout the Old Testament that you can look up if you want to see that God has always had a heart for the whole world (Genesis 14, Exodus 18, Numbers 22–24, Numbers 32:12, Joshua 2, Judges 3:9, Judges 3:31, Judges 4–5, the entire book of Ruth, 2 Samuel 11–12, 1 Kings 17, 2 Kings 5, the book of Job [probably], Jonah 1:16, and Jonah 3). Also, look up verses like Exodus 12:48–49, Numbers 9:14, and Numbers 15:13–16. The prophets of the Old Testament, and God himself, often had something to say about the Gentiles (non-Israelites). Jonah was literally commissioned to go *to* a Gentile city to save it from destruction by turning its people back to God. What was his reason for running from said commission? He knew God would have mercy on an enemy city if they turned to him. Jonah 4:1–3 says,

> But it displeased Jonah exceedingly, and he was angry. And he prayed to the Yahweh and said, "Yahweh, is not this what I said when I was yet in my country? That is why I made haste to flee to Tarshish; for I knew that you are a gracious God and merciful, slow to anger and abounding in steadfast love, and relenting from disaster. Therefore now, Yahweh, please take my life from me, for it is better for me to die than to live."

Jonah fled because he *wanted* Ninevah destroyed so much that he would rather *die* than live with the knowledge that he played a part in the salvation of the city. He knew God would not destroy them if he preached to them and they believed. The Ninevites were not God's chosen people, yet they were saved when they turned to him.

The next big argument from the Calvinistic side against Arminianism is that if God just has foreknowledge of who would choose him and then God chooses those people because he knows that they will choose him, then he loses his sovereignty. That is correct. In that instance, God does lose his sovereignty, which is why it's not true. God does indeed have foreknowledge of who will choose him, but God calls *all* to him instead of just choosing those whom he knows will choose him. Only those who go through his chosen way to him (via his Son's death and resurrection) become his chosen ones.

Human Choice Has *Always* Played a Role

Whenever the Bible talks about salvation or following God, it specifically talks about choices made by individuals. Let me give a couple of quick examples. Matthew 16:24 (NIV) says, "Then Jesus said to his disciples, 'Whoever *wants* to be my disciple, must *deny themselves* and *take up their cross and follow me*'" (emphasis added). Matthew 19:21 says, "Jesus said to him, 'If you would be perfect, go, sell what you possess and give to the poor, and you will have treasure in heaven; *and come, follow me*'" (emphasis added). One would be hard-pressed to find examples of salvific verses that do *not* include human choice.

More broadly speaking, in the Old Testament, God didn't specifically call the Gentiles, yet some still came to him. As seen above, the Ninevites in the book of Jonah is an excellent example of this, as is Rahab and many others. However, in the New Testament, God called the Jews, and the vast majority didn't come to him. Therefore, God was angry with them and sent a call out to all the people of the earth to come to him. This is shown in the parable of the great banquet in Luke 14:16–24 which says,

> But he [Jesus] said to him, "A man once gave a great banquet and invited many. And at the time for the banquet he sent his servant to say to those who had been invited, 'Come, for everything is now ready.' But they all alike began to make excuses. The first said to him, 'I have bought a field, and I must go out and see it. Please have me excused.' And another said, 'I have bought five yoke of oxen, and I go to examine them. Please have me excused.' And another said, 'I have married a wife, and therefore cannot come.' So the servant came and

reported these things to his master. Then the master of the house became angry and said to his servant, 'Go out quickly to the streets and lanes of the city, and bring in the poor and crippled and blind and lame.' And the servant said, 'Sir, what you commanded has been done, and still there is room.' And the master said to the servant, 'Go out to the highways and hedges and compel people to come in, that my house may be filled. For I tell you, none of those men who were invited shall taste my banquet.'"

God called his people to him and they rejected him. Clearly, God's sovereign choice does not override human choice. The parable above tells of sovereign choice and human choice working together for salvation.

Another example is the parable of the sower in Matthew 13. The sower is anyone who spreads the Word of God. They sow seed all over. On rocky ground, among thorns, on the path, and on good soil, they sow the seed that is the message about the kingdom of heaven to all. The seed that falls on the rocky ground is like those who hear the Word of God and receive it with joy, but because their roots do not go deep, they fail to last. The seed that falls among the thorns is like those who hear the Word of God, but the worries of life choke them and make them fruitless. The seed that falls on the path never takes root and is snatched away by Satan because they didn't understand the Word of God, but the seed that lands on the good soil is like those who understand the Word of God. Their roots go deep, and they produce much fruit. This is why we must spread the gospel. We are the sowers. Romans 10:15 says, "How beautiful are the feet of those who preach the good news!" God prepares the soil, but he uses believers to spread the good news to the ends of the earth.

Can God sow as well? Of course, and in fact, he does. The very universe that we live in cries out to all humans showing them the glory of God (Psalm 19:1). God can also directly intervene as he did with Paul before he was called Paul. However, God never forces us to choose him. We always have a choice to go against him because love isn't love without choice, and worship is a poor imitation if it is forced. That is the very reason Adam and Eve had the choice in the first place. If God only wanted people to worship him even if they didn't have a choice, then the Garden of Eden would not have included forbidden fruit. Instead, God chose to have mankind as a free agent who could choose to follow him or go against him. Even Paul who saw the glory of God to the point where it blinded him, could have said no if he wanted to. After all, is that not exactly what Satan did? He was made by God, lived with him, and saw him in all his glory and yet still decided to rebel against God.

God is also *always* preparing the soil of people's hearts so that the seed can take root in their hearts and grow when they hear the good news. We are enslaved to lies until God begins to tear down those lies. He makes a way for that seed of the gospel to reach our dead hearts so that we can catch even a glimpse of who he is—a glimpse of truth. He cultivates that seed, but without us being willing to let him work the soil like he wants to, the seed cannot grow. It is our choice to let God work effectively in our lives. We must believe he is who he says he is, and what Jesus has done for us. We must follow him. When we do that, God makes us into a new creation, giving us a heart of flesh instead of stone. The seed has sprouted, and a new creation has come out of it.

Against Calvinism

Up to this point, I have tried to be fairly equitable regarding my attempt to lay out what Scripture teaches on election. However, now I wish to move onto a different track and address Calvinism, or the reformed tradition. While I agree that there are issues with Arminianism, they are not as problematic as the issues presented by Calvinism. As such, when limited in space, it is more important to address the side with greater problems. Not addressing Arminianism does not constitute agreement with the view on my part. Additionally, I have not done an exhaustive study into Calvin's teachings. However, I am of the opinion that his teachings were much less controversial than modern versions, similar to Arminius. Calvinism is arguably the result of many theologians' thoughts, not only John Calvin's work.[1] As such, my argument is against the contemporary treatment of Calvinism rather than against Calvin himself.

Before I dive into the problems I see with the Calvinistic view of the doctrine of election, I want to clarify one point. Some of what you will see below is what I believe is the logical conclusion of the doctrine from an objective angle. I would argue that, in most cases, the practical way Calvinism is played out does not align with what the doctrine lays out logically. This is a good thing as you will find that I am quite harsh with my objections to this doctrine. Since the practical ways that the doctrine is handled are significantly different than its logical conclusions, I am still able to hold most Calvinists as my brothers and sisters in Christ. If the doctrine was lived out as it logically concludes, I am not so sure that this

---

1. Richard A. Muller *After Calvin: Studies in the Development of a Theological Tradition* (New York: Oxford University Press, 2003), 8.

would be the case (hence the "Against Calvinism" critique). With that said, I am going to address the problems that I see with the Calvinistic doctrine of election. What are the consequences/applications of holding to the view that I have since demonstrated as unbiblical?

- There is no need to evangelize.

John S. Feinberg, a Calvinistic theologian, discusses this critique in his book *No One Like Him: The Doctrine of God*. He notes, initially, how if God chooses who will be saved without input from humans (the Calvinistic view), "Calvinism, then, seems to cut the nerve of evangelism."[2] His ensuing argument against this idea does nothing to help his case.[3] To begin with, he tries to flip the script by arguing that someone who believes in libertarian free will might become discouraged since there may be no more people willing to freely turn to God since God does not force anyone to come to him. This person could work relentlessly and give up due to not seeing any fruit from their labor. Conversely, Calvinists are nearly *guaranteed* to find fruitful mission grounds. To argue for this, Feinberg states,

> On a Calvinistic understanding, however, there is reason to witness. Our witness may be the means to someone's salvation, and if not, God can still use our testimony in our life to perform valuable things. Beyond that, believing that there

---

2. Feinberg, *No One Like Him*, 702.

3. This is an extremely common theme. Calvinists tend to make the same, or similar, arguments against this idea, but the arguments fail to help, as I hope to demonstrate.

are elect who haven't yet been saved, we can be enthusiastic about the enterprise of missions. Even if our witness is not the means to others coming to Christ, it is dubious that no missionary efforts will bear fruit.[4]

He continues by demonstrating that the reason "it is dubious that no missionary efforts will bear fruit" is that Revelation shows there will still be people being saved even into the Tribulation. Thus, a Calvinist can expect to find elect people now.

There are a couple of problems with this line of reasoning and what he wrote. First, this last part is also true of those who believe in libertarian free will. Scripture clearly shows that there will still be people getting saved in the end times, thus a free-will advocate can reasonably make the same argument as Feinberg.

Second, Feinberg didn't address the problem. He wrote of how a Calvinist's witness "may be the means to someone's salvation" even though this is exactly the problem. If the Calvinistic doctrine of election is correct, God is saving the elect regardless of what anyone else does. A Calvinist does not need to do anything! Nor *can* he do anything. That's the whole problem with the doctrine! At no point does a Calvinist's witness to someone matter. It *cannot*. Otherwise, something other than God played a role in salvation. This is something that they vehemently reject.

Additionally, the very fact that we have "unreached" people groups argues against what Feinberg and other Calvinists argue. Consider the following image:

---

4. Ibid., 704. This is also argued by J. I. Packer on page 106 of his book *Evangelism and the Sovereignty of God*.

(A full color image is available at The Joshua Project website.)

Why are most of the unreached people groups in Africa, the Middle East, and Asia? Do Calvinists really want to argue that entire groups of people or nations are not elect? If Calvinism is true, then we should not see unreached people groups. There should, theoretically, be a better spread of elect around the world, even in places where Christians have little to no influence. Yet, based on the image above, it seems like only certain people groups are elect while others are not. What does God have against all the others? Does he sovereignly reject Northern Africans, Middle Easterners, and Southern Asians or does human choice play a role in salvation? The latter seems much more likely, especially when we add in everything we learned in the first major section of this chapter. These regions are both highly religious and tend to be hostile to Christians. Therefore, it makes more sense that they are exercising their free will in rejecting God—by following false gods—than that God is sovereignly not choosing them.

Some attempt to work around the lack of a need to evangelize by saying that it is an honor to participate in God's work, however, this is just as pointless. If God is the only one who makes any form of decision on who gets to come to him, then we simply do not need to evangelize. The problem we run into is that God *commands* us to evangelize on *many* occasions. The Great Commission found at the end of Matthew 28 is an excellent example of this. Additionally, Paul wrote in Romans 10:13–17:

> For "everyone who calls on the name of the Lord will be saved." How then will they call on him in whom they have not believed? And how are they to believe in him of whom they have never heard? And how are they to hear without someone preaching? And how are they to preach unless they are sent? As it is written, "How beautiful are the feet of those who preach the good news!" But they have not all obeyed the gospel. For Isaiah says, "Lord, who has believed what he has heard from us?" So faith comes from hearing, and hearing through the word of Christ.

This is just a couple of chapters after the "proof" text of Calvinist predestination. Scripture tells us that we have a major part to play in regard to salvation. People cannot be saved by faith in Jesus if they have never heard of Jesus. That is why we *must* evangelize. But Calvinism teaches a different means of salvation. It teaches a salvation that doesn't require "calling on the name of the Lord to be saved." It instead teaches that God simply chooses whom he will save. I will address this particular idea in greater depth later on.

Finally, the fact the Calvinists *do* evangelize, quite a lot I might add, does *not* detract from the fact that their *teaching* makes evangelism pointless. This fact (that Calvinists evangelize a lot) is often the defense given to this argument that I have just laid out.[5] However, this simply means that they practice what they do not teach which, in this case, is a *good* thing.

- It allows for, and even encourages, lukewarm Christians.

If God sovereignly chooses who can come to him and who can't, what's the point of living a righteous life? Why not just live a life full of sin? You can have your cake and eat it too. In this sense, Calvinism has the same problem the "sinner's prayer" has. They can, and are, both used as a way of getting out of the need to live righteously. Calvinism is arguably *worse* than the sinner's prayer though. At least the sinner's prayer forces one to recognize their sinfulness and need for Jesus. Calvinism says you are either doomed or saved based entirely on someone else's choice. Thus, regardless of whether you are God's elect, you have no need to live a righteous life. It simply doesn't matter if you are elect or not.

- It often produces arrogant, aggressive, and obnoxious Christians.

Within Calvinism, there is something called a "cage-stage Calvinist." I am going to quote R. C. Sproul on this simply to demonstrate that Calvin-

---

5. See, for example, Timothy George's *Theology of the Reformers*. On page 176 of the 2013 version, he demonstrates that those who hold to the Calvinistic view of predestination (or a very similar version) are often some of the most ardent evangelists.

ists are well aware of this problem within their ranks. In a ligonior.org article called "Escaping the 'Cage Stage,'" Sproul said,

> My friend Michael Horton often comments on the phenomenon of "cage-stage Calvinism," that strange malady that seems to afflict so many people who have just seen the truth of the Reformed doctrines of grace. We've all known one of these "cage-stage Calvinists." Many of us were even one of them when we were first convinced of God's sovereignty in salvation.[6]

He goes on to discuss how newly converted Reformed believers often turn every discussion into an "argument for limited atonement or for making it their personal mission to ensure everyone they know hears—often quite loudly—the truths of divine election."[7] Basically, they are so aggressive for their newfound beliefs that they should be locked in a cage until they can cool down and mature a bit. Now, I can only speculate as to why this is (Sproul gives a reason in the article, but it seems shallow to me), but I do know that this is not how *any* Christian should be presenting themselves. Why is it so common for Calvinists to be this way? The fact that there is a phrase for this *within the community* is significant. It indicates that there may be something else at play. What exactly? I don't know. From the two previous points, there shouldn't be *any* desire to force this doctrine on others, yet that is exactly what we are seeing. This arrogance

---

6. R. C. Sproul, "Escaping the 'Cage Stage,'" Ligonier Ministries, November 25, 2013, https://www.ligonier.org/learn/articles/escaping-cage-stage

7. Ibid.

and aggression is counter to basically everything a Christian is supposed to be. If any other doctrine were to produce this kind of reaction in those who believe in it, we would seriously question the doctrine. Something *has* to be off for a teaching to consistently produce this kind of person. Seriously, what other doctrine regularly produces this kind of result? Was John Wesley correct when he stated that this doctrine was the "hellish doctrine" in his hymn?

> Thou has compell'd the Lost to die;
> Hast reprobated from thy Face;
> Hast Others sav'd, but them past by;
> Or mock'd with only Damning Grace.
> How long, thou jealous God, how long
> Shall impious Worms thy Word disprove,
> Thy Justice stain, thy Mercy wrong,
> Deny thy Faithfulness and Love.
> ***Still shall the Hellish Doctrine stand?***
> And Thee for its dire Author claim?
> No—let it sink at thy Command
> Down to the Pit from whence it came.[8]

Am I convinced that this is a "hellish doctrine?" I am not sure. As I said previously, I do not think that Calvinists actually live according to the teaching that they uphold. It does seriously disconcert me though to see a doctrine so consistently produce a person who even those who teach

---

8. John Wesley, "On God's Everlasting Love," in *Arminian Magazine 1* (1778): 432. (emphasis added).

the doctrine believe should be locked in a cage until they have a chance to mature. It is a major red flag.

- There is a lot of cherry-picking of verses and passages.

Are there verses that teach what a Calvinist teaches? Absolutely. However, they aren't meant to be taken alone. There are *a lot* of passages that focus on salvation throughout Scripture. Calvinism ignores a good half of them, or at least de-emphasizes that half. This is a type of cherry-picking. Cherry-picking is a dangerous practice. Instead of trying to figure out how the verses on God's sovereign choice *and* verses on man's choice work together, Calvinists will focus almost exclusively on the former.[9] The best way to understand what the Bible teaches on something is to find every possible verse or passage that addresses said topic. Then, each of these passages needs to be evaluated in light of each other and God's character as seen throughout Scripture. In this case, there are contradictory verses, or at least they are contradictory if one holds to the Calvinistic view of election and God's sovereignty. That said, these passages *cannot* contradict each other if, indeed, they are truly God's Word. We must align ourselves to Scripture and not make Scripture fit our own desires and theology.

- Jesus' death on the cross is pointless.

If God is going to save those whom he wills regardless of their belief in him, then Jesus didn't need to die. After all, isn't the fact that God *requires*

---

9. Conversely, Arminians run the risk of doing exactly the same thing by over-emphasizing the verses on human choice. We *must not* do this with any doctrine! Over-emphasizing anything results in false doctrine.

a perfect sacrifice a sign that he isn't truly sovereign, at least from a Calvinist's definition? Shouldn't a sovereign God be able to simply decree that someone is righteous? Couldn't he keep them from sinning throughout their lives and thus have no need for Jesus to sacrifice himself? God *should* be able to do this unless there is more at play here. Of course, there *is* more at play here. God *cannot* forgive sin without a sacrificial payment. Blood is owed when a man sins, either his own or a valid substitute. In the Old Testament, this involved animal sacrifices. A human had to recognize their sin and then be obedient to God by rending their hearts and turning back to him, but they also needed to offer a sacrifice to take their place. The same is true today. The difference is that there is a once and for all sacrifice. Jesus offered himself, in obedience to the Father, as a willing and perfect sacrifice able to cleanse the world of its sins if we but repent and turn to him. Now he sits on the throne in glory. The problem is simply that all of this would not have been necessary if God could divinely choose people apart from their will and regardless of their sin.

- Finally, the Calvinistic doctrine of election teaches a different God.

Our God, though sovereign, doesn't desire or need people to love him by force which is precisely what is taught in Calvinism. From the very beginning, God has given us a choice: Follow him or go our own way. Calvinism doesn't allow for this. It teaches about a God who doesn't care about whether we actually desire to be with him. Yet, even in Genesis 1 and 2, we simply don't see this. God desires a relationship with those who obey him willingly. He *wants* us to choose him above all else. Not only that, but he gives us authority. He gave man authority over all the earth. The God of Calvinism would never do this. That is an attack on his sovereignty, at least the Calvinistic view of sovereignty.

Similarly, the logical end of a God like this is that God himself is, ultimately, evil and the source of sin and evil. Even some Calvinists know this and make arguments for it! As far as I am aware, no Calvinistic theologians argue that God is evil; however, there are some who argue that God ordains sin and evil. For example, Edwin H. Palmer writes, "It is even biblical to say that God has foreordained sin."[10] This is a *huge* problem. If God *ordains* sin or is its *source* or *cause*, then God is sinful and evil. When true free will is removed from the equation, God becomes the author of sin. He is no longer the good and perfect God of Scripture (see, for example, Mark 10:18 and Psalm 18:13). In *Debating Calvinism*, Dave Hunt notes, "Intending to protect God's sovereignty, Calvinism makes Him the cause of every thought, word, and deed, and thus of sin."[11]

If we accept the Calvinistic view of sovereignty, we are left with a God who willingly chooses to send most of those who were made in his image to hell. Pastor Ronnie W. Rogers writes,

> Calvinism asks us to believe that God chose eternal torment for the vast majority of His creation (Matthew 7:13–14). They want us to rejoice in a God who desires and chose for

---

10. Edwin H. Palmer, *The Five Points of Calvinism: A Study Guide* (Grand Rapids, MI: Baker Books, 2010), 100.

11. Dave Hunt and James White, *Debating Calvinism: Five Points, Two Views* (Colorado Springs, CO: Multnomah Books, 2004), 335.

the vast majority of his creation to go to hell when He could have redeemed them.[12]

This is not something I can rejoice in, nor do I see it in Scripture. The biblical view of God is one who has done everything short of forcing us to follow him. He created us in his image to be like him (Genesis 1:26–27), gave us his Word (2 Timothy 3:16), sent his Son to *die* in *our place* though his Son begged him for another way (Matthew 26:39), commissioned his followers to go and make more disciples (Matthew 28:19), and now waits patiently to execute judgment on the world. Why does he wait? Because he does not wish "any should perish, but that all should reach repentance" (2 Peter 3:9). This verse flies in the face of Calvinism and is sufficient on its own to reject it outright; however, it is not alone. Many verses argue against God's supposed desire to subject his creation to eternal torment simply because he chose it.

Ultimately, based on the above discussion, this conclusion can be made: Calvinism adherents teach a false gospel and a false God yet do not *follow* a false gospel and God. It is really a "do as I do, not as I say" doctrine. Again, this is a good thing considering that actually adhering to what is taught by Calvinism leads to a false god and a false gospel. A Calvinist who truly adheres to the tenets of his faith is lost while believing he is found.

---

12. Ronnie W. Rogers, *Reflections of a Disenchanted Calvinist: The Disquieting Realities of Calvinism* (Bloomington, IN: WestBow Press, 2016), 26.

A Brief Call to Action

If you found value in this book, please consider leaving an honest review on your favorite book review site (Amazon, BookBub, Goodreads, etc.). Reviews are tremendously helpful to authors. They are, in many ways, the lifeblood of a book and I highly appreciate each one that I receive.

Also, if you are interested in receiving updates on books, book reviews, and other short teachings that I publish, you can follow me on:

- Facebook (Meta): L. J. Anderson at www.facebook.com/profile.php?id=61553506423559

- YouTube: L. J. Anderson at www.youtube.com/@ljandersonbooks

- My website: www.ljandersonbooks.com

ALSO BY L. J. ANDERSON

Short Books

*Theology and Apologetics: An Examination of
How and Where They Intersect*

Books

Salvation by Faith Alone? Living in the Nuance of Faith and Works
(coming soon!)

Once Saved Always Saved? A Refutation of the Doctrine of Eternal Security
(coming soon!)

BIBLIOGRAPHY

Adams, Jay E. *Handbook of Church Discipline: A Right and Privilege of Every Church Member.* Grand Rapids, MI: Zondervan, 1986.

Akin, Daniel L., David S. Dockery, and Nathan A. Finn, eds. *A Handbook of Theology.* Brentwood, TN: B&H Academic, 2023.

Allison, Gregg R. *The Baker Compact Dictionary of Theological Terms.* Grand Rapids, MI: Baker Books, 2016.

Allison, Gregg R. *Sojourners and Strangers: The Doctrine of the Church.* Wheaton, IL: Crossway, 2012.

Andrew, Stephen L. "Biblical Inerrancy." *Chafer Theological Seminary Journal* 8.1 (Winter 2002): 1-20.

Baggett, David, and Jerry L. Walls. *The Moral Argument: A History.* New York: Oxford University Press, 2019.

Beale, Gregory K. *The Erosion of Inerrancy in Evangelicalism: Responding to New Challenges to Biblical Authority.* Wheaton, IL: Crossway Books, 2008.

Behr, John. *Irenaeus of Lyons: Identifying Christianity.* Oxford: Oxford University Press, 2013.

Blomberg, Craig. *Can We Still Believe the Bible? An Evangelical Engagement with Contemporary Questions.* Grand Rapids, MI: Brazos Press, 2014.

Bradley, Raymond S. *Paleoclimatology: Reconstructing Climates of the Quaternary.* Amsterdam: Elsevier, 1999.

Campbell, Dylan. "Aristotle's On the Heavens." *World History Encyclopedia.* October 16, 2016. https://www.worldhistory.org/article/959/aristotles-on-the-heavens/.

Carlton, Wynne. "Inerrancy is Not Enough: A Lesson in Epistemology from Clark Pinnock on Scripture," *Unio cum Christo* 2, no. 2 (October 2016): 67-81.

Clinton, Tim, and Ron Hawkins. *The Quick Reference Guide to Biblical Counseling: Personal and Emotional Issues.* Grand Rapids, MI: Baker Books, 2009.

Cook, David. *Understanding Jihad.* Berkeley: University of California Press, 2015.

Cragun, Rodger L. *The Ultimate Heresy: The Doctrine of Biblical Inerrancy.* Eugene, Oregon: Wipf & Stock Publishers, 2018.

Craig, William Lane. *Reasonable Faith: Christian Truth and Apologetics.* Wheaton, IL: Crossway, 2008.

Craig, William Lane, and J. P. Moreland, eds. *The Blackwell Companion to Natural Theology.* Malden, MA: Wiley-Blackwell, 2012.

Curry, Oliver Scott, Daniel Austin Mullins, and Harvey Whitehouse. "Is It Good to Cooperate? Testing the Theory of Morality-as-Cooperation in 60 Societies." *Current Anthropology* 60:1 (2019): 47-69.

Diamond, Lisa M., and Molly Butterworth. "Questioning Gender and Sexual Identity: Dynamic Links over Time." *Sex Roles*, 59 (5–6): 365–376. doi:10.1007/s11199-008-9425-3.

Dunham, Kyle C. "The Role of Biblical Creationism in Presuppositional Apologetics." *Detroit Baptist Seminary Journal*, 25 (2020): 3–29.

Ehrman, Bart D. *Lost Scriptures: Books That Did Not Make It into the New Testament.* Oxford: Oxford University Press, 2003.

Engel, Alexander. "'In This World Nothing Can Be Said to Be Certain, except Death and Taxes' Benjamin Franklin, 1789." *Colorectal Disease*, April 1, 2012. https://doi.org/10.1111/j.1463-1318.2012.03001.x.

Erikson, Millard. *Christian Theology.* Grand Rapids, MI: Baker Academic, 2013.

BIBLIOGRAPHY

"Escaping the 'Cage Stage'" by R.C. Sproul. Ligonier Ministries. November 25, 2013. https://www.ligonier.org/learn/articles/escaping-cage-stage.

Feinberg, John S. *No One Like Him: The Doctrine of God.* Wheaton, IL: Crossway, 2005.

Frame, John M. "Inerrancy: A Place to Live." *Journal of the Evangelical Theological Society* 57, no.1 (03, 2014): 29-39.

France, R. T. *Matthew: An Introduction and* Commentary. Downers Grove, IL: InterVarsity Press, 1985.

Geisler, Norman L. *Christian Ethics: Contemporary Issues & Options.* Grand Rapids, MI: Baker Academic, 2010.

Glueck, Nelson. *Rivers in the Desert: A History of the Negev.* New York: Grove Press, 1959.

Gould, Paul M., Travis Dickinson, and R. Keith Loftin. *Stand Firm: Apologetics and the Brilliance of the Gospel*. Nashville, TN: B&H Academics, 2018.

Grant, Robert M. *Irenaeus of Lyons*. London: Routledge, 1996.

Grudem, Wayne, *1 Peter: An Introduction and Commentary.* Downers Grove, IL: InterVarsity Press, 1988.

Grudem, Wayne. *Systematic Theology: An Introduction to Biblical Doctrine*. Grand Rapids, MI: Zondervan Academic, 2020.

Guthrie, Donald. *The Pastoral Epistles: An Introduction and Commentary*. Downers Grove, IL: InterVarsity Press, 1990.

Hammett, John S. *Biblical Foundations for Baptist Churches: A Contemporary Ecclesiology*. Grand Rapids, MI: Kregel Publications, 2005.

Hammatt, John S., and Benjamin L. Merkle, eds. *Those Who Must Give an Account: A Study of Church Membership and Church Discipline*. Nashville, TN: B&H Academic, 2012.

Hazen, Robert M. "How Old Is Earth, and How Do We Know?" *Evo Edu Outreach* 3. May 26, 2010. https://evolution-outreach.biomedcentral.com/articles/10.1007/s12052-010-0226-0.

Heckel, Matthew C. "Is R. C. Sproul Wrong About Martin Luther? An Analysis of R. C. Sproul's *Faith Alone: The Evangelical Doctrine of Justification* with Respect to Augustine, Luther, Calvin, and Catholic Luther Scholarship." *Journal of the Evangelical Theological Society* 47, no. 1 (Mar 2004): 89-120. https://www.proquest.com/scholarly-journals/is-r-c-sproul-wrong-about-martin-luther-analysis/docview/211214959/se-2.

Hodge, Bodie. "Harvard, Yale, Princeton, Oxford—Once Christian?" *Answers Magazine*. June 27, 2007. https://answersingenesis.org/christianity/harvard-yale-princeton-oxford-once-christian/.

Hogan-Doran, Justin. "Case Analysis: Murder as a Crime Under International Law and the Statute of the International Criminal Tribunal for the Former Yugoslavia: Of Law, Legal Language, and a Comparative Approach to Legal Meaning." *Leiden Journal of International Law* 11 (1998): 165-181.

Hunt, Dave, and James White. *Debating Calvinism: Five Points, Two Views*. Colorado Springs, CO: Multnomah Books, 2004.

Iricinschi, Eduard, et al. *Beyond the Gnostic Gospels: Studies Building on the Work of Elaine Pagels.* Tübingen: Mohr Siebeck, 2013.

Jastrow, Robert. *God and the Astronomers.* New York: W. W. Norton and Company, 1992.

Johnson, Keith L. *Theology as Discipleship*. Downers Grove, IL: InterVarsity Press, 2015.

Kimble, Jeremy M. *40 Questions About Church Membership and Discipline.* Grand Rapids, MI: Kregel Academic, 2017.

Kratt, Dale Eugene. "The Secular Moral Project and the Moral Argument for God: A Brief Synopsis History." *Religions* 14, no. 8 (2023): 982-1004.

Leeman, Jonathan. *Church Discipline: How the Church Protects the Name of Jesus.* Wheaton, IL: Crossway, 2012.

Leeman, Jonathan. *Understanding Church Discipline.* Nashville, TN: B&H Books, 2016.

Lewis, C. S. *Mere Christianity.* New York: HarperOne, 1952.

Loke, Andrew Ter Ern. "A New Moral Argument for the Existence of God." *International Journal for Philosophy of Religion* 93, no. 1 (February 2023): 25-38, https://www.proquest.com/scholarly-journals/new-moral-argument-existence-god/docview/2777940980/se-2.

MacArthur, John, ed. *The Inerrant Word: Biblical, Historical, Theological, and Pastoral Perspectives.* Wheaton, IL: Crossway, 2016.

Massey, Lesly F. "Biblical Inerrancy: An Anxious Reaction to Perceived Threat," *Pennsylvania Literary Journal* 13, no. 1 (Spring, 2021): 100-120, 342. https://www.progquest.com/scholarly-journals/biblical-inerrancy-anxious-reaction-perceived-docview/2536820699/se-2.

McGregor, Kirk R. "Biblical Inerrancy, Church Discipline, and the Mennonite-Amish Split." *Journal of the Evangelical Theological Society* 60, no. 3 (September 2017): 581-593. https://www.proquest.com/scholarly-journals/biblical-inerrancy-church-discipline-mennonite/docview/1964554361/se-2.

McGrath, Alister. *Christianity's Dangerous Idea: The Protestant Revolution-A History from the Sixteenth Century to the Twenty-First.* New York, NY: HarperCollins Publishers, 2007.

Mcleod, Saul. "Humanistic Approach in Psychology (Humanism): Definition & Examples." *Simply Psychology*. December 20, 2023. https://www.simplypsychology.org/humanistic.html.

Mohler, R. Albert, et al. *Five Views on Biblical Inerrancy*, ed. J. Merrick and Stephen M. Garrett. Grand Rapids, MI: Zondervan, 2013.

Moreland, J. P. *Love Your God with All Your Mind: The Role of Reason in the Life of the Soul.* Colorado Springs, CO: NavPress, 2012.

Morris, Leon. *1 Corinthians: An Introduction and Commentary.* Downers Grove, IL: InterVarsity Press, 1985.

Moser, Paul K., and Paul Copan, eds. *The Rationality of Theism*. New York: Routledge, 2003.

Muller, Richard A. *After Calvin: Studies in the Development of a Theological Tradition.* New York: Oxford University Press, 2003.

Naselli, Andrew David. "What the New Testament Teaches About Divorce and Remarriage." *Detroit Baptist Seminary Journal* 24 (2019): 3-44.

Olson, Roger E. *Arminian Theology: Myths and Realities.* Downers Grove, IL: InterVarsity Press, 2006.

Palmer, Edwin H. *The Five Points of Calvinism: A Study Guide.* Grand Rapids, MI: Baker Books, 2010.

Pagels, Elaine H. "'The Mystery of the Resurrection': A Gnostic Reading of 1 Corinthians 15." *Journal of Biblical Literature* 93, no. 2 (1974): 276-288. https://doi.org/10.2307/3263097.

Patterson, Stephen J., James M. Robinson, and Hans-Gebhard Bethge. *The Fifth Gospel: The Gospel of Thomas Comes of Age.* London: T & T Clark, 2011.

Porter, Stanley E., and David I. Yoon. *Paul and Gnosis.* Leiden, Netherlands: Brill, 2016.

Poythress, Vern S. *Inerrancy and the Gospels: A God-Centered Approach to the Challenges of Harmonization.* Wheaton, IL: Crossway, 2012.

Ratzsch, Del. *Science and Its Limits: The Natural Sciences in Christian Perspective.* Downers Grove, IL: InterVarsity Press, 2009.

Rogers, Ronnie W. *Reflections of a Disenchanted Calvinist: The Disquieting Realities of Calvinism.* Bloomington, IN: WestBow Press, 2016.

Runzo, Joseph. "God, Commitment, and Other Faiths: Pluralism vs. Relativism," *Faith and Philosophy.* 5 (1988): 343–364.

Sagan, Carl, et al., *Cosmos: A Personal Journey.* Studio City, CA: Cosmos Studies, 2000.

Scharping, Nathaniel. "Gravitational Waves Show How Fast the Universe Is Expanding." *Astronomy*. October 18, 2017. https://www.astronomy.com/science/gravitational-waves-show-how-fast-the-universe-is-expanding/.

Shrock, Christopher A. "Mere Christianity and the Moral Argument for the Existence of God." *Sehnsucht: The C. S. Lewis Journal* 11, no. 1 (2023): 99-120. https://web.p.ebscohost.com/ehost/pdfviewer/pdfviewer?vid=3&sid=9fffc152-0aac-427a-9b3a-e71bbc550d02%40redis.

Sproul, R. C. (Robert Charles). *Faith Alone: The Evangelical Doctrine of Justification*. Grand Rapids, MI: Baker Books, 1995.

Sweis, Khaldoun A. and Chad V. Meister. *Christian Apologetics: An Anthology of Primary Sources*. Grand Rapids, MI: Zondervan, 2012.

"The Chicago Statement on Biblical Inerrancy." *Evangelical Review of Theology*, 4, no. 1 (1980).

Treier, Daniel J., and Walter A. Elwell, eds. *Evangelical Dictionary of Theology*. Grand Rapids, MI: Baker Academic, 2017.

Vanhoozer, Kevin J. "Lost in Interpretation? Truth, Scripture, and Hermeneutics." *Journal of the Evangelical Theological Society* 48, no. 1 (March 2005): 89-114. https://www.proquest.com/scholarly-journals/lost-interpretation-truth-scripture-hermeneutics1/docview/211221919/se-2.

Vanhoozer, Kevin J. "The Semantics of Biblical Literature: Truth and Scripture's Diverse Literary Forms," in D.A. Carson and John Woodbridge (eds.), *Hermeneutics, Authority, and Canon* (1986): 49-104.

Voosen, Paul. "2.7-Million-Year-Old Ice Opens Window on Past," *Science*, August 18, 2017. https://www.science.org/doi/10.1126/science.357.6352.630

Wesley, John. "On God's Everlasting Love," *Arminian Magazine 1* (1778): 432.

Weaver, C. Douglas, and Rady Roldán-Figueroa. *Exploring Christian Heritage: A Reader in History and Theology.* Waco, TX: Baylor University Press, 2017.

Witte Jr., John. *The Blessings of Liberty: Human Rights and Religious Freedom in the Western Legal Tradition.* Cambridge: Cambridge University Press, 2021.

Zacharias, H. Daniel, and Benjamin K. Forrest. *Surviving and Thriving in Seminary: An Academic and Spiritual Handbook.* Bellingham, WA: Lexham Press, 2017.